LIFEAFTERMANZANAR

LIFE AFTER MANZANAR

Naomi Hirahara and Heather C. Lindquist

Foreword by Art Hansen

Heyday, Berkeley, California

Manzanar History Association, Independence, California

This project was funded in part by a grant from the U.S. Department of the Interior, National Park Service, Japanese American Confinement Sites Grant Program. The views and conclusions contained in this document are those of the authors and should not be interpreted as representing the opinions or policies of the U.S. government. Mention of trade names or commercial products does not constitute their endorsement by the U.S. government.

The publishers wish to thank The Blue Family Charitable Fund and The Kagawa Family Charitable Fund, as well as individual donors, for their generous support of this project.

Library of Congress Cataloging-in-Publication Data is available.

Cover photo by Stone Ishimaru. Courtesy of The Bancroft Library, University of California, Berkeley. © Tec Com Productions

The family of Ichisuke and Ume Fukuhara, originally from Santa Monica, California, left Manzanar War Relocation Center and temporarily resettled in Farmingdale, Long Island. Here they are posed with their new friends, the Olsen family, outside their house on the grounds of the Calderone Greenhouses. Standing (*left to right*) are son Willy, Ichisuke, daughter Tomiko, Ume, daughter-in-law Fujiko, and Henry Fukuhara, Fujiko's husband, who is holding their younger daughter, Yoshino. Among those seated is their older daughter, Shizuko.

Book design by Rebecca LeGates

Orders, inquiries, and correspondence should be addressed to:
 Heyday
 P.O. Box 9145, Berkeley, CA 94709
 (510) 549-3564, Fax (510) 549-1889
 www.heydaybooks.com

Printed by Jostens in Visalia, CA

10 9 8 7 6 5 4 3 2 1

This book is dedicated to Maggie Wittenburg, former executive director of Manzanar History Association, and Jim Howell, a former National Park Service park guide. Maggie began volunteering for Manzanar History Association in 2003, and over the years, she rose to the role of executive director. Jim began working as a seasonal ranger for Manzanar in 2010, followed by a stint at Tule Lake and a second season at Manzanar. Maggie recruited Jim to work as a researcher for this book, and he did so, refusing to accept pay. For both Maggie and Jim, this book was a labor of love, not only because of the important lessons it has to teach but for the opportunity it gave them to collaborate. They shared a passion for history and for preserving the stories and lessons of Manzanar, but, unfortunately, they also shared a journey neither could have imagined when this book project began. Both were diagnosed with pancreatic cancer in late 2016 and died within six weeks of each other—Maggie in December 2016 and Jim in January 2017. We wish they could be here to see the results of their vision and work. We were honored to work with them and believe they would be honored by the final product of their efforts.

—Alisa Lynch, chief of interpretation,
Manzanar National Historic Site, National Park Service

Below, left to right: Bob Takamoto, Bruce Sansui, and Mas Ooka revisit Manzanar, July 2016. *Right:* Bob, Bruce, and Mas as boys, growing up behind barbed wire, c. 1944.

In 1942, the United States government ordered more than 110,000 men, women, and children to leave their homes and detained them in remote, military-style camps. Two-thirds of them were born in America. Not one was convicted of espionage or sabotage.—Introductory text to the Visitor Center exhibition at Manzanar National Park

What becomes "history" and from whose point of view? How do you encourage people to explore its dark chapters and come away even stronger? Why remember when you would just as soon forget?—Karen Ishizuka in *Lost and Found: Reclaiming the Japanese American Incarceration*

CONTENTS

FOREWORD

Following Japan's attack on the Pearl Harbor naval base in the United States territory of Hawai'i on December 7, 1941, the U.S. government removed some 120,000 people of Japanese ancestry—about two-thirds of them American citizens, the remainder Japan-born aliens banned by law from achieving U.S. citizenship—from their homes on the West Coast and beyond, confining them in American-style concentration camps.

Historically, the World War II experience of people of Japanese descent (Nikkei) was referred to euphemistically as an "evacuation" or incorrectly as an "internment." Recently, however, it has been characterized more realistically, if still too restrictively, as an "incarceration." Perhaps, though, it would most accurately be designated a "social disaster." Striking with as much force and devastation as some natural disasters, the wartime catastrophe that befell the Japanese Americans was entirely human-made, the result of racism, exploitation, improper government leadership, and lack of public vigil.

The U.S. government's stated rationale for the enforced mass uprooting and incarceration of Japanese Americans was military necessity and national security. Under the guise of keeping the nation safe from its enemies, Nikkei Americans were removed from their homes and communities and consigned for the duration of the war to remote and crude detention facilities located in windblown deserts and boggy forests of the country's interior.

The first of these detention facilities was Manzanar, which made it the flagship and prototype for all the others that followed in its wake. It was located outside West Coast military zones in eastern California's Inyo County, 212 miles north of Los Angeles and nearly halfway between the Owens Valley towns of Lone Pine and Independence, on U.S. Highway 395. Before the 1860s, the Manzanar site had been home for centuries to Paiute and Shoshone Indians. They were displaced by homesteaders, who in turn sold out to developer George Chaffey in the early 1900s. Chaffey planted fruit trees, subdivided the property into small ranches, and marketed it as Manzanar (Spanish for "apple orchard"). By 1930, the orchard owners had sold the land to the Los Angeles Department of Water and Power.

The Manzanar camp was established initially by the U.S. Army as an "assembly center," and from March 21 through May 31, 1942, it was managed by the Wartime Civil Control Administration (WCCA) as the Owens Valley Reception Center. On June 1, 1942, Manzanar became the only one of fifteen total "assembly centers" to be reconstituted as a relocation center administered by the War Relocation Authority (WRA), and it was renamed Manzanar War Relocation Center. As a WCCA unit, Manzanar had one project director (Clayton Triggs) and two acting directors (Solon Kimball and Harvey Coverley). In its "relocation center" phase, which extended to its shutdown on November 21, 1945, Manzanar's two directors were Roy Nash (until November 24, 1942) and Ralph P. Merritt. The overwhelming majority of the camp's peak population of 10,046 (nearly equally divided between male and female, with one-quarter of them school-age children) derived primarily from prewar Japanese American communities in Los Angeles County, particularly the city of Los Angeles, which was the prewar population, commercial, and sociocultural capital of mainland Japanese America.

Situated in the rain shadow of the imposing Sierra Nevada range at the base of 14,375-foot Mount Williamson on some 6,000 acres of land leased from the Los Angeles Department of Water and Power, Manzanar was known for its harsh climate of extreme temperatures, high winds, and severe dust storms. The camp proper consisted of a 550-acre rectangle dominated by thirty-six blocks of 504 tar-papered residential barracks for the incarcerated population, most of whom lived within twenty-by-twenty-five-foot family apartments. This area encompassed communal mess halls, laundry facilities, and latrines for each inmate block, as well as considerably upgraded living facilities for the appointed personnel. Additionally, it contained a modern 250-bed hospital, schools, churches, recreational and cultural facilities, cooperative stores, and most other amenities—including a newspaper—that one would expect to find in a "normal" American city of comparable size. Also in this central area were war-related industries (for example, a camouflage-net factory), an experimental plantation for producing natural rubber from the guayule plant, and the Children's Village orphanage. Immediately outside the main camp were 1,500 acres of agricultural land, which not only contributed to Manzanar's food supplies but also augmented those of several of the nine other WRA camps. The camp's core was surrounded by barbed wire and overlooked by eight sentry towers and manned by armed military police, a battalion of whom was quartered a half-mile south of the Manzanar center and, in 1942, was equipped with twenty-one rifles, eighty-nine shotguns, six machine guns, and twenty-one submachine guns.

I first visited the Manzanar site in 1972 when I accompanied a close friend and colleague from the history department at California State University, Fullerton (CSUF), Kinji Ken Yada, on the occasion of his commemoration of the time thirty years previous when he, then an adolescent Nisei (second-generation Japanese American), together with his Issei (immigrant-generation Japanese American) parents exchanged their prewar residence in Los Angeles's Little Tokyo for a barracks apartment in Manzanar. This pilgrimage so powerfully impacted me that I decided to shift my major field of historical research and publication from Anglo-American intellectual history to the World War II Japanese American eviction and detention experience.

Within the next two years I took steps to solidify this transformation. First, I launched the Japanese American Project in CSUF's Oral History Program. Second, I coordinated a lecture series on the World War II Japanese American exclusion and confinement story that included two speakers prominently identified with the Manzanar story, Sue Kunitomi Embrey and Togo Tanaka (both featured in *Life after Manzanar*). Third, I coedited a Japanese American Project book with Betty Mitson, *Voices Long Silent*, which amounted to an oral-historical inquiry into assorted dimensions of the Manzanar experience. Fourth, I tape-recorded in-depth interviews for the CSUF Japanese American Project with noteworthy Manzanarians, including not only the aforementioned Embrey and Tanaka but also two of Manzanar's Caucasian assistant directors, an inmate policeman, an inmate dentist, an inmate from Washington's Bainbridge Island, the inmate Communist couple Karl and Elaine Yoneda, and an array of non–Japanese American wartime residents in the Owens Valley towns proximate to Manzanar. Fifth, I attended my first Manzanar pilgrimage with others who visit the site annually to remember and reflect. Finally, I coauthored an article, "The Manzanar Riot," which interpreted the bloody events of early December 1942 (duly recorded in the pages of this book) as a "revolt" rather than a "riot."

Thereafter, I redirected my research away from Manzanar per se to explore inmate resistance activity within all ten of the WRA detention centers. However, I still maintained a special interest in Manzanar, and over the years I have consulted on Manzanar-related books and documentary films, assisted Manzanar National Historic Site (MNHS) in variable ways, coedited an annotated bibliography on the site, keynoted a Manzanar pilgrimage, presented a Day of Remembrance talk at the site, and nurtured an oral history volume, *Twice Orphaned*, on the Children's Village at Manzanar. On one occasion, I combined my Manzanar and camp resistance interests via a coauthored book, *Manzanar Martyr*, the centerpiece for which was the oral-historical memoir of Harry Ueno, the pivotal figure in the so-called Manzanar riot.

The marriage between Manzanar and resistance is precisely why I find Naomi Hirahara and Heather Lindquist's *Life after Manzanar* so altogether captivating. Although their research burden in relationship to Manzanar is primarily focused on the aftermath of that camp's inmate population and only tangentially on their wartime site experiences, I would argue that resistance to oppression is nonetheless the leitmotif of their remarkable book.

Before commenting further on *Life after Manzanar*, it should be noted here that after the Manzanar riot—which galvanized the inmate population in mass dissent against the oppressive actions of the U.S. government and the WRA, abetted by the collaborationist role played by the Japanese American Citizens League leaders—there occurred in Manzanar in 1943 a still more protracted and pervasive show of inmate protest. It was set in motion in February, when the army and the government imposed a mandatory registration of the adult population of Manzanar (and the other WRA centers) for the joint purpose of establishing eligibility for leave clearance and securing volunteers for a special segregated Japanese American combat team. At Manzanar, only 42 persons (2 percent of the eligible citizen males) volunteered for military service, while approximately 50 percent of all male citizens and 45 percent of all female citizens originally either answered "no" to the so-called loyalty questions on the registration questionnaire or refused to answer the questions. (These percentages dropped to 27 percent of male citizens and 21 percent of female citizens when respondents were given the opportunity to change their answers.) The latter situation led to 1,322 allegedly "disloyal" Manzanarians and their families (a grand total of 2,165 individuals) being transferred in late 1943 to the WRA's newly established Tule Lake Segregation Center in Northern California.

For the remaining two war years, Manzanar was a more accommodating camp. Thus, in early 1944, when the War Department's resumption of the Nisei draft was challenged by a widespread inmate resistance movement, it was one of only two WRA camps (the other was Gila River in Arizona) not to log a solitary draft resister. With the departure of its "disloyals" to Tule Lake and an increasing number of its "loyals" entering the military and resettling throughout the United States as war workers and college students, Manzanar became a community largely of elderly and young residents.

Having been involved in designing the exhibits in MNHS's superb interpretive museum, Hirahara and Lindquist are acutely cognizant of Manzanar's entire history and legacy. Thus, in the comparatively brief compass of four chapters—all resourcefully documented and enhanced by a diverse array of historical photographs, illustrations, and callouts—they have succeeded brilliantly in relating the core post–World War II Japanese American story as perceived through the lens of strategic journeys undertaken by a judiciously selected cast of individuals and families who were wartime Manzanar inmates.

The opening chapter of *Life after Manzanar* features the phenomenon of Japanese American "resettlement," which began in 1942 and, some would argue, extended into the mid-1960s (and even beyond). In spite of a few notable recent studies on this topic, it has largely remained a woefully neglected middle link between "relocation" and "redress" in Japanese America's narrative chain, both in scholarly literature and in popular memory. This neglect, which in 1980 sociologist Tetsuden Kashima labeled "social amnesia," has not been salutary. It has fostered the false understanding in the mainstream American public that, notwithstanding their wartime mistreatment, the Nikkei metamorphosed almost instantly after World War II into a "model minority." This misperception cleanses the "relocation" of its status as a bona fide social disaster, replete with long-lasting dislocations and repercussions, and reduces the painstaking rebuilding by Nikkei individuals, families, groups, and communities during the postwar years to a puzzling miracle of race, ethnicity, and culture. It is, therefore, one of the foremost attainments of the present study that the resettlement experience of Manzanarians is accorded proper and long-overdue attention.

While the theme of resistance to oppression is present throughout Hirahara and Lindquist's resettlement chapter, it assumes center stage in *Life after Manzanar*'s subsequent chapters. All three revolve around redressing the conditions and factors that led to the demonization and detention of Japanese Americans during World War II, and all of them in addition highlight the decisive part played by select Manzanarians in the reform and revitalization process that began in the 1950s and 1960s, gained traction and momentum over the following two decades, and culminated in the passage of the Civil Liberties Act of 1988.

It is highly instructive both actually and symbolically to note that in the pan–Japanese American movement that precipitated the passage of this act—which apologized for the grave injustice done to Americans of Japanese ancestry during World War II, established a public education fund to prevent future offenses directed toward other Americans, and awarded reparation payments of $20,000 to each incarceration survivor—the three principal redress organizations (the National Council for Japanese American Redress, the Japanese American Citizens League, and the National Coalition for Redress/Reparations) were headed up by former Manzanarians: William Hohri, a camp teenager; John Tateishi, a camp infant; and Alan Nishio, who was born in camp.

Clearly, the Manzanar legacy of dissent, protest, and resistance was at work within and through these three men, as well as through other men and women both inside and outside Manzanar. In reading *Life after Manzanar*, it should also be readily apparent to readers that this legacy has been keenly comprehended and exquisitely captured by the volume's two exceedingly gifted authors.

Art Hansen
October 2017

CHAPTER ONE

THE GATES WERE CLOSED AFTER US

It was Wednesday, November 21, 1945, the day before Thanksgiving. The month had been cool in Manzanar War Relocation Center, with low temperatures in the twenties. Forty-nine people made their way to the front gate through a grid of abandoned barracks, mess halls, and latrines—structures that had at the camp's peak been used by 10,046 Japanese Americans, including immigrants, long-term residents, and citizens. These forty-nine people were the last of those who had been brought to this remote site in California's Owens Valley in cars, buses, and trains—the windows covered—from scattered parts of the state and even as far away as Bainbridge Island, Washington. Guilty only of having Japanese ancestry while the United States was fighting Japan in World War II, they hadn't known what was in store for them when they arrived in 1942 at the concentration camp at the foot of the Sierra Nevada range.

Now, three years later, the last of these families to depart were again unsure of what lay ahead. One of the remaining incarcerees now leaving at last was Shinjo Nagatomi, the camp's lead Buddhist

From September to November 1945, more than a thousand people left Manzanar each month; by mid-November, only a few hundred remained.

Rev. Shinjo Nagatomi at Manzanar, c. 1945.

minister, who had arrived in Manzanar in August 1942, having been transferred there from Tanforan Assembly Center, located near the family's residence in San Francisco. He was there with his wife, Sumi, and their three young daughters, Hideko, twelve, Shizuko, eight, and Manzanar-born Shinobu, now two. They could have left the camp earlier, when the Reverend Nagatomi had been assigned to work with a True Pure Land (Jodo Shinshu) Buddhist temple in Southern California, but the minister had declined to leave at that time. He wanted to stay until he could make sure the very last—the other forty-four—were safely released.

Most of those who stayed until the bitter end—especially the very last ones—simply didn't have other options. As much as they might have wanted to leave, once they were released, where could they go? Most likely they didn't have property to return to, and perhaps they didn't have well-connected friends who could help them resettle. Some were elderly, and others were sick or were caring for sick family members, including infants who had been born in camp. Even the orphans that had been kept in the Manzanar Children's Village had been placed in foster homes by then.

The camp authorities had been releasing waves of incarcerees since as early as June of 1942, and those who were able to leave usually did. Among the first to be released were Nisei young adults—the children

As the last people to leave Manzanar vacate their barracks "homes," all that remains are empty crates, abandoned ponds and gardens, discarded personal belongings, and enduring memories.

of first-generation immigrants, known as Issei. Approximately four thousand from all ten camps left for colleges and jobs in the Midwest or on the East Coast, thanks to the aid of the Quaker-led American Friends Service Committee (AFSC), and later the National Japanese American Student Relocation Council (NJASRC). After being investigated and cleared on an individual basis, they were granted leave clearance as long as they had a sponsor and agreed to disperse further into the nation's interior east of the Rocky Mountains.

Many of these young Nisei men and women agreed with the sentiments of Togo Tanaka, who said, "We had one objective: We wanted to get the hell out of there." Togo, a brilliant UCLA graduate and English editor of the *Rafu Shimpo* newspaper in Los Angeles, was incarcerated at Manzanar with his wife and young daughter. "We were dying of anxiety, neurosis, and frustration from seeing the

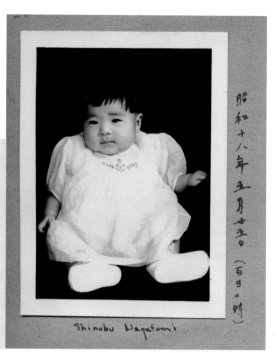

昭和十八年五月廿五日（百日の時）

Shinobu Nagatomi

Right: Shinobu (Jean) Nagatomi, one of 541 babies born in Manzanar, 1943.

Below: The last picture of the Nagatomi sisters before leaving Manzanar, 1945. *Left to right*: Shizuko (Shirley); Shinobu (Jean), clutching her sister's beloved Jeannie Walker doll; and Hideko (Dee).

barbed wire and watchtowers," he said in an interview for an oral history project.[1] "There wasn't [a] day when I didn't try to figure out some way to get out of there."

In November of 1945, it was finally time for the Nagatomis to go, and they were ready. Their luggage easily fit into the station wagon that was to transport them because, according to Shizuko (now known as Shirley), they didn't have much. Her most treasured possession had been a Jeannie Walker doll that her younger sister had ruined by combing out its hair. Most of their other belongings had been sent ahead to the Gardena Buddhist Church, including not just furniture and housewares but also precious heirlooms and even the boxes containing the cremated remains of family members who had died in camp.

As these "last ones" were released, each received twenty-five dollars and a one-way bus ticket to make a new life outside Manzanar. Project director Ralph P. Merritt marked the moment with an impromptu speech and sent them on their way.

"The gates were closed after us," said Shirley. "I still remember the loud clang of the gate closing as the station wagon drove off. Off to the free world."

The car turned right on Highway 395, leaving behind camp and the only structures they had known for the past few years. Besides the barracks and abandoned gardens, there was the cemetery's stark white obelisk, which featured the Japanese word *ireito* (慰霊塔), meaning "In memory of the deceased." Rev. Nagatomi had prepared the original calligraphy that others had then carved into the cemetery tower.

---

1. Togo Tanaka's interview was conducted in 1973 as part of the Japanese American Oral History Project at California State University, Fullerton. Sources for the quotes from other former incarcerees can be found in the bibliography at the back of this book.

MANZANAR CHILDREN'S VILLAGE

Six-year-old Annie Shiraishi Sakamoto and nine-year-old Celeste Loi Teodor were two of the last orphans to leave Manzanar's Children's Village in August 1945, and although they weren't particularly close at the time, life after camp would bring them together and forge a lifelong bond. One of the things they had in common was a traumatic departure from camp: the Children's Village at Manzanar had been the only home that Annie could remember, and Celeste recalls it as having been a surprisingly pleasant oasis. "I absolutely loved it there," she said. "The only bad memory I had was when I had to leave. We all cried our eyes out." Annie recalled their long bus ride back to Los Angeles, her face "pressed against the window . . . wondering Where are they taking us and What's going to happen to us?"

Like many of the other 101 Japanese American children who were tossed together in the Children's Village, the orphanage that served all ten camps, Annie and Celeste were truly defenseless and alone in the world. They had no legal guardians, and their only advocates were the harried and overworked staff of the Children's Village and the government social workers from outside camp gates. In the rush to move these youngest Japanese Americans into the camps in the first place, vital papers—including birth certificates and addresses of parents and closest living relatives—often went missing and the children became lost in the system. According to social worker Helen Whitney, who visited Manzanar in 1945, the War Relocation Authority maintained that the Children's Village was "no more than a boarding home for [the children] until they can be properly placed or otherwise provided for," but wartime and camp conditions understandably made that especially difficult.

Some children were adopted into loving homes and families—the parents included both former incarcerees and non-Japanese individuals—while others came of age at Manzanar and eventually found

Wilma Stuart *(above right)* was the temporary foster mother of Annie Shiraishi Sakamoto *(above left)* for two years, starting in August 1945. Celeste Loi Teodor *(right, with her husband, Peter)* was also under Stuart's care after being released from Manzanar.

their way in the world as young adults without the support and care of a family. Once the war ended and the camps closed, many children became wards of the counties to which they were returned, while others entered the foster care system, like Annie and Celeste, who became foster sisters for a while and friends for life.

Leaving camp was also hard on the staff of volunteers who worked to make the Children's Village a warm and loving place for its young charges. Jack Takayanagi was attending art school in Los Angeles before the war started, and while incarcerated at Manzanar he not only helped out at the Children's Village—also called Shonien, the name of a Japanese American orphanage in Los Angeles—he

Newlyweds Jack and Mary Takayanagi, Des Moines, Iowa, July 1944.

also planned various religious activities, including Manzanar's first Christmas Eve service. Jack was just nineteen years old and he had recently undergone a Christian spiritual awakening that was to influence his path going forward. When the Christmas service was in danger of being canceled due to an encroaching sandstorm, he thought to himself, "In the midst of this storm of Manzanar, we will seek a faith that will carry us through."

Jack was intent on leaving camp and pursuing his religious education, and in 1943, through the help of both the AFSC and his girlfriend's sister, who was studying at Drake University in Des Moines, Iowa, he was accepted into the school's liberal arts program. Most emotionally wrenching was saying goodbye to the Shonien children. Jack walked down to the gate, passing two sentries, and crossed to the other side of the highway to catch a red Santa Fe bus. "As I stood there, Mary [his girlfriend], my mother, and [my] dad were standing on the other side. And up the way a little bit were the Shonien kids who had come, and they were all pressing against the barbed wire fence. And I could see them.

"When the bus came, I got on the bus and walked to the back of the bus to get the back seat so I could look out the window. They were all waving. The Shonien kids particularly were all pressed against the barbed wire fence, waving. And I said, 'As long as I'm alive and have the energy, this will never happen again.'" At that moment, young Jack committed his life to a ministry of justice. He married his high school sweetheart, Mary, later that year and the couple settled into a new life in the Midwest.

RESETTLEMENT IN LOS ANGELES COUNTY

What kind of "free world" would confront the Nagatomis and the others finally leaving camp? Even though the war was over, many communities were still hostile to anyone who looked like "the enemy," and California already had a running list of terrorist incidents targeting people of Japanese ancestry. In a confidential report to Dillon S. Myer, director of the War Relocation Authority (WRA), the incidents had been divided into the following categories: attempts of shooting and dynamiting, arson, threatening visits, and intimidation. And these, of course, were only the incidents that had been documented.

Most of the reported crimes took place in California's Central Valley, but incidents were happening all over the state. Near the border of Compton, in Los Angeles County, John Takahashi suffered at least two incidents of vandalism and intimidation, including having the window of his home broken with stones in June 1945, which came just three months after his window had been smashed with an iron pipe. In the Los Angeles suburb of Gardena, where the Nagatomis were headed, Joe Kobata, a pioneering flower grower, became a victim

Archie Miyatake and traveling companions stop in the Mojave Desert en route to Los Angeles. *Left to right:* Archie Miyatake, Tomoji Mori (the owner of the truck), and Chizuko and Mike Nishida, 1945.

of arson when someone set fire to the cheesecloth that shaded the half acre of chrysanthemum blooms in his nursery. The flowers were burned, and the WRA field officer noted, "The crop may be ruined."

Before World War II, one-third of those incarcerated in WRA concentration camps had come from Los Angeles County. As they were released, the goal of the WRA was to disperse them throughout the country rather than allow them to be "bunched up as groups," in the words of WRA director Myer. As part of his postwar assimilation plan, he hoped that no more than half of the released inmates would return to the West Coast, thereby "moving to the liquidation of a most difficult minority problem."[2] Still, whether he liked it or not, California would need to prepare for the return of Japanese Americans, and Myer held several special meetings and released press statements as a way of assuaging the fears of those who were less than enthusiastic about the reemergence of Japanese Americans in their neighborhoods. He publicly clashed with Los Angeles Police Department Commissioner Al Cohn over the WRA's policy to not issue special identification for Japanese Americans returning to the West Coast. According to the *Los Angeles Times*, Myer stated that he did not believe those released from camps should "continually be forced to produce credentials." He also refused to release to local authorities the names and addresses of returning Japanese Americans. Rebutting critics who feared for their safety and security with the imminent arrival of resettlers from various camps, Myer affirmed, "Military intelligence and FBI records show that not once since Pearl Harbor have Americans of Japanese ancestry, either here or in Hawai'i, been proved as engaging in espionage or sabotage."

Discrimination fueled during the war was still high (if not higher) when Japanese Americans reintegrated into society. Even a Japanese man wearing a U.S. military uniform could become a target of racist insults and threats. One returning Nisei soldier who had served a tour of duty overseas with the Military Intelligence Service remembers being called a "damn Jap" while riding the bus one day. Fortunately,

---

2. Dillon Myer made this statement in a town hall meeting in Los Angeles on January 21, 1944.

the bus driver, also a veteran, defended the man and told the passenger, "Lady, apologize to this American soldier or get off my bus."

By June 1945, only eleven hundred Japanese Americans had chosen to return to Los Angeles County—compared to the thirty-seven thousand who had been forced to leave—but that number grew slowly and steadily over time. Hank Umemoto was sixteen years old when he moved into a residential hotel on Skid Row with his mother and sister. In his memoir, *Manzanar to Mount Whitney,* he described it as "a room that was nine by twelve and furnished with amenities including a cold water washbasin in one corner, a single community toilet at the end of the hall for over half a dozen families, and a bathtub door that opened upon request." Still a teenager, and having been relatively sheltered during the years he had spent in camp, he suddenly found himself stepping over drunkards and passing prostitutes and brothels on his walk to school.

For Hank, this post-camp life was more challenging than being at Manzanar. "It was not the struggle for survival, but it was a struggle to be accepted into the American mainstream," he wrote. In one of many recollections of the discrimination he faced, he remembers being denied entry into movie theaters and being

The Japs Must Not Come Back!

by Lambert Schuyler

25 cents

Above: Anti–Japanese American pamphlet, "The Japs Must Not Come Back!," 1944.

Below: Hank Umemoto on Skid Row in Los Angeles, 1948.

sequestered to a bench next to the toilet on a train, despite the car being virtually empty. "I wished that I was born anything else but a Japanese," Umemoto said, adding that this "darker side" of the Nisei experience—this lack of self-worth—is often something those who suffer from it keep to themselves.

When the Nagatomis finally reached their new home on the grounds of the Gardena Buddhist Church on 166th Street, they found a rat-infested house. It wasn't luxurious, but it provided a roof over their heads, and even at eight years old Shirley knew they had it much better than many others, even those staying elsewhere on temple property. In the neighboring buildings, conditions were not unlike the barracks at Manzanar and the nine other concentration camps that had held Japanese Americans during the war years. Multiple families were sharing spaces they had separated into makeshift rooms by hanging blankets as partitions for the least amount of privacy.

In September 1945, the Gardena Buddhist Church's sanctuary and its language school had been converted into a hostel, and many other Japanese American churches and community centers throughout the state were providing temporary shelter for former incarcerees.

The most well known was the Evergreen Hostel at the Japanese Union Church at 506 N. Evergreen Avenue in the historic Los Angeles neighborhood of Boyle Heights, just east of Little Tokyo. Sponsored by the AFSC and the Presbyterian Church, the Evergreen Hostel had the capacity to hold one hundred people, although it housed many more than that in its first three months of operation. This and seven other hostels under the same coalition charged a standard rate of one dollar per day, with slight adjustments made for length

Rev. Shinjo Nagatomi and his daughters soon after their arrival in Gardena, California, 1945.

Above, left to right: Henry Suenaga, from Manzanar, and Ben Nishiyama, from Poston, photographed by Charles E. Mace in one of the men's dormitories at Los Angeles's Evergreen Hostel, June 1945.

Below: Evergreen Hostel, Boyle Heights, Los Angeles, 1945. Photo by Marion Palfi.

of stay, income, and number of dependents.[3]

It was in one of these hostels that eighteen-year-old Mary Kageyama, known as the Songbird of Manzanar, married Shiro "Shi" Nomura, twenty-five. The two had officially met in 1944, when Shi escorted Mary to one of the events sponsored by his Manza-knights Club, a social organization for young adults in Manzanar. Shi apparently had known of Mary and her musical talent before World War II, but being in camp together gave him the opportunity to get to know the young singer. "By the time I left camp in January [1945], we were already prom-ised to each other," Mary recalled in an oral history interview conducted in 2009.

Mary and her siblings had been cleared by the government to leave camp and move to Pasadena, California, where her eldest brother, Frank, was able to parlay his experience working on a groundbreaking camp project to produce guayule, a natural rubber, into a job at Caltech.

3. Jeffrey C. Copeland, "Stay for a Dollar a Day: California's Church Hostels and Sup-port during the Japanese American Eviction and Resettlement, 1942–1947" (M.A. thesis, University of Nevada, Reno, 2014).

Mary Kageyama (*standing*) and her younger sister Tillie (*seated*) relocated to Pasadena with their older brother Frank in January 1945. Soon after this picture was taken by Charles E. Mace, Mary, the Songbird of Manzanar, became engaged to Shiro Nomura.

A few months later, Shi was able to leave camp as well, and in June 1945 their wedding was held at the AFSC hostel in Pasadena. Herbert Nicholson, a Quaker minister who had conducted some of the Christian services in Manzanar and was one of the most high-profile non-Japanese advocates for the Japanese American community, presided over the Nomura nuptials.

Another non-Japanese leader—and in fact the only non-Japanese minister in the Jodo Shinshu sect of Buddhism—was the Reverend Julius Goldwater, a cousin of the politician Barry Goldwater. He presided over three temples that opened their doors to homeless Japanese Americans during and after the war. He had known the Nagatomi family from before the war, and Shirley remembered him once visiting their house in San Francisco. "It was the first white man I had seen in our home," she said.

In addition to the Gardena Buddhist Church, Goldwater took care of the Senshin Buddhist Temple and the Los Angeles Hompa

Hongwanji, more popularly known as Nishi Hongwanji, a meeting place in Little Tokyo that had in 1942 been a site from which Japanese Americans were taken by bus to detention facilities. (It is now the location of the Go for Broke National Education Center.) Many of their belongings had been stored at the temple during the war.

Between 1942 and 1945, Goldwater rented out empty space in Nishi Hongwanji to the Providence Baptist Association (PBA), a predominantly African American group.[4] This transaction was one of many that led to the wholesale transformation of Little Tokyo into an African American community during World War II. In fact, the new residential and business district was dubbed Bronzeville, and the name became familiar enough that by 1943 the residents had established a Bronzeville Chamber of Commerce. The black newcomers came from the Deep South to answer the defense industry's increased demand for laborers in the port city of Los Angeles. While the work was there, however, housing was not. In light of the region's racial covenants and discriminatory housing policies, these newcomers needed shelter, and Little Tokyo was conveniently empty of its ten thousand Japanese American residents and business owners. In a year's time, the population of Bronzeville reached at least twenty-five thousand, with people cramming into not only official residences but also vacant storefronts, garages, and makeshift living quarters. According to researcher Martha Nakagawa, who created the Bronzeville–Little Tokyo history website at http://bronzeville-la.ltsc.org, it was not uncommon for sixteen people to live in one room and forty people to share one bathroom. The men who worked twenty-four-hour shifts in defense plants were known to rent space to sleep—known as "hot beds"—on a rotating schedule. This around-the-clock schedule also led to a vibrant nightlife and the rise of what were called "breakfast clubs"—popular meeting places that stayed open until the wee morning hours. Jazz

---

4. According to an article by Michihiro Ama titled "Multiracial Buddhist Lawsuits in Postwar Los Angeles," the PBA sublet some rooms at the temple to the physician George H. Hodel, Jr., who later gained notoriety (albeit posthumously) when his son, Steve, a detective for the Los Angeles Police Department, accused him of the gruesome 1947 murder of a young woman who came to be known as the Black Dahlia. He was one of the prime suspects but fled the country before he could be charged with the crime.

Crowded wartime housing in Bronzeville, Los Angeles, 1943.

legend Charlie Parker performed in Bronzeville clubs during this era, and celebrity customers included Judy Garland and Gene Kelly.

The vast majority of Bronzeville's residents rented or squatted in the vacant properties, but some individuals, including Bronzeville pioneer Leonard Christmas, actually purchased real estate. In 1943, Christmas became the first African American to run a business in Bronzeville when he bought the hundred-room Digby Hotel at 506½ East First Street, on the corner of Alameda and First Streets. Another enterprising citizen, Clara Brown, came to Bronzeville from New Orleans and led a cooperative enterprise of nineteen black women who turned a former Japanese business into the "first Negro department store in the Far West."[5] The vast majority of the properties were either owned by white landlords or left abandoned when their Japanese American landlords were incarcerated.

Just as Nishi Hongwanji had been rented to the Providence Baptist Church (and to another religious organization, the First Street Baptist Institute), the Japanese-owned Centenary Methodist Church became the home of black-owned Trinity Baptist Church; and Union Church, the impressive structure on North San Pedro Street, was eventually

---

5. Scott Kurashige, *The Shifting Grounds of Race: Black and Japanese Americans in the Making of Multiethnic Los Angeles* (Princeton, NJ: Princeton University Press, 2008).

used by the Pilgrim House, which was established to provide social services to mitigate the problems created by overcrowding.

Contrary to dire predictions by city politicians that race riots would erupt when Japanese Americans were released from the camps to, presumably, resettle in their old neighborhoods, nothing like that transpired. Community groups such as the Common Grounds Committee sought to forge good relations between the new African American residents and the returning Japanese Americans, and among the media outlets that hoped to foster peaceful relations between the two populations was the *California Eagle* newspaper, which served the African American community. It took up the mantle to advocate for a fellow disenfranchised minority, in part by announcing a new editorial policy to eliminate use of the slur "Jap" on its pages.

Many incarcerated families were able to eventually return to the general areas they had left, but it wasn't easy, even for those whose prewar homes were still intact. Many homeowners felt compelled to turn their residences into to makeshift hostels, and Bob Miyatake,

A shoeshine shop in Bronzeville, Los Angeles, 1946.

Three generations of the Azeka family outside Baby House Cleaners, in Bronzeville/ Little Tokyo, 1952.

the second son of renowned Manzanar photographer Toyo Miyatake, recalled that at one time more than twenty people lived in his family's modest home in the multiethnic Los Angeles neighborhood of Boyle Heights.

Aside from securing housing, the other major challenge for the resettlers was finding work. The prospect was especially disheartening for those who had been successful business owners before the war and now had to start over from scratch, as was the case of the Azeka family. Before the war they had operated a laundry business in the Uptown area of Los Angeles (now Koreatown), and as they prepared to reenter that business, the patriarch, Jenyemon Azeka, set his sights on Little Tokyo. For $200 he was able to buy Baby House Cleaners, at 341½ East First Street, from an African American businessman. Next door were a black-owned barbershop and shoeshine parlor.

The third-youngest Azeka daughter, Sumiko, remembers having to work at the cleaners as a teenager—steaming wrinkles from wholesale bundles, ironing, and checking in clothes. With laundry fees around

People protest local labor practices, including sweatshop conditions, on the streets of Bronzville, 1946.

fifteen cents per piece of clothing, such services were affordable for the working person, and their customers reflected the demographics of the changing neighborhood: both African American and Japanese American.

Over time, Little Tokyo returned to its prewar incarnation as a Japanese American community, but the transition was not seamless or without some tense moments. Goldwater's Nishi Hongwanji had a host of troubles, starting in 1945, when the Providence Baptist Association sued for alleged "forcible entry" during the time the property was being transferred back to the Japanese American congregation. Then, in 1947, the temple sued its own Rev. Goldwater, who was accused of mishandling temple funds. After losing the suit, he left the sect to become a nonaffiliated Buddhist teacher.

The fragile biracial coalitions and relationships did not have much time to develop; for the most part, as the Japanese Americans moved back in, the African Americans moved out. The end of the war brought an end to many defense-industry jobs held by African Americans in Bronzeville, and the residents dispersed to other parts of the city, the state, and the country. Bronzeville, vibrant as it was, was short-lived and soon became a distant memory and little more than a blip in Los Angeles history.

"REPRESENTATIVE AND TALENTED NISEI"

Bright Sierra sunshine cast a dark shadow behind Chico Sakaguchi when Dorothea Lange, one of several documentary photographers working for the WRA, photographed her on July 3, 1942.

Chico was the lone English major among the family's seven siblings, most of whom had heeded their mother's advice to get out of the family truck farming business and become doctors. Mary, one of Chico's younger sisters, was the first in the family to leave Manzanar, departing

Chico Sakaguchi, as photographed by Dorothea Lange at Manzanar, 1942.

in April 1943 to complete her medical training at the Women's Medical College in Philadelphia. Chico followed the next year, having secured employment as a teacher. By then, the WRA's Photographic Section (WRAPS) was actively documenting—and aggressively promoting—resettlement.

Soon after her arrival in Philadelphia, Chico was featured as a "representative and talented Nisei" in a series of WRAPS photographs. The purpose of these and thousands of similar photos was to encourage other Nisei to strike out on their own to the Midwest or East Coast, often as defense or agricultural workers, or to continue their educations. The photos also served to convince potential resettlement communities that the newcomers were solid, law-abiding American citizens.

Less than a year after leaving Manzanar, however, Chico died— alone and far away from her loved ones. (By then, her sister Mary had left Philadelphia to complete anatomy coursework in Salt Lake City.) While working at the Hope Day Nursery School in Philadelphia,

Chico was hospitalized for asthma and died from an accidentally high dose of adrenaline. Mary said she "died because of the camp," believing Manzanar's dust had exacerbated Chico's allergies. According to her older brother Sanbo, when she got to camp, the allergies "turned into asthma."

For the Sakaguchi family, Chico's death in February 1945 was part of a larger cascade of loss. In the space of one year, the family patriarch, Shiichiro, died from throat cancer; the eldest son, Obo, died from stomach cancer; and the middle daughter, Lily Sakaguchi Thibodeaux, suffered a nervous breakdown. Over the course of that year, Sanbo—who had not been incarcerated with his family because he was already enrolled in medical school in the Midwest—traveled a total of ten thousand miles to attend family funerals and to collect his sister's ashes.

Although Chico and Obo didn't survive the resettlement years long enough to fulfill the promise (or carry the burden) of becoming what WRAPS called "representative and talented Nisei," their brothers and sisters did. After returning to the Los Angeles area, Mary and Sanbo, with the help of Lily, ran a successful medical practice together in the San Fernando Valley, while two other Sakaguchi brothers, Bo and Chebo, worked for decades as dentists.

Above left: Members of the Sakaguchi family in North Hollywood, California, August 10, 1935.
Above right: Chico Sakaguchi and children at Hope Day Nursery, Philadelphia, July 1944.

RESETTLEMENT IN THE MIDWEST

At first the government's strategy to move Nisei into the interior of the United States had been successful. Many went to the largest city in the Midwest, Chicago, which before World War II had been home to only about four hundred Japanese American residents. By 1945–46 there were twenty thousand. Just as the influx of African Americans from the Deep South had completely transformed Los Angeles's Little Tokyo, the stream of Japanese Americans impacted urban Chicago. Although there were exceptions, most Japanese Americans lived in one of two neighborhoods in the Windy City: one was near the Northside area, around Clark and Division Streets, and the other one was on the Southside, in the neighboring Oakland and Kenwood communities.

Former journalist Togo Tanaka and his family were among the first resettlers to arrive in Chicago. In Manzanar, Tanaka was a historical documentarian for the War Relocation Authority (WRA). When tensions in the camp led to a confrontation between Japanese Americans and military police on December 6, 1942, leaving two young Japanese Americans dead, Tanaka, perceived as an informant for the administration, was in danger. Four days later, he and his family, including most of his extended relatives, as well as several dozen others, were herded away to an abandoned former Civilian Conservation Corps camp in Death Valley.

Moving from confinement in Manzanar to confinement in Death Valley, Tanaka was desperate to "get out of living behind barbed wire, and having soldiers escort us everywhere we go." He was determined to accept the first legitimate job offer that came his way. That job ended up being a staff position with the Midwest office of the AFSC, which was responsible for helping resettle Japanese Americans in Chicago.

Togo, his wife, Jean, and daughter, Jeannie, were sent to live at the AFSC hostel at 350 West Belden Avenue on the Northside, about a mile and a half from downtown's landmark Loop.

As the Tanakas, their suitcases in hand, took the streetcar from the train station, a stranger pointed to a building on the street. "See that garage?" the passenger said. "That's where the Capone gang had lined up and massacred the gangsters." As soon as the Tanakas moved into the hostel, Togo suggested they walk two blocks and visit the notorious garage. "The people who occupied the garage knew all about it," he remembered. They took us in and showed us where the blood spots were. But that was Chicago. We knew we were in new territory."

Tanaka soon discovered that while a number of churches and social service agencies had stepped up to receive the released Japanese Americans, the infrastructure was weak and assistance was haphazard. Before the WRA had even devised an official relocation plan, the city's YWCA offered housing to "young women resettlers," becoming one of the first agencies to meet the rapidly expanding need.

By the time the Tanakas arrived, various social service agencies had joined forces under an Advisory Committee for Evacuees, but Togo observed that it was indeed only advisory and often couldn't solve the more practical problems of resettlement. As it turned out, the AFSC did the bulk of the early work, and when the WRA stepped in later, it was on the receiving end of much pent-up frustration. Togo, who worked for the AFSC but was nevertheless somewhat sympathetic to the struggles of the government agency, noted that "absence of a well-defined program" was "characteristic of every resettlement agency

Togo Tanaka and his wife, Jean Miho Tanaka, as photographed by Dorothea Lange at Manzanar, July 1942.

in Chicago," but he also underscored the impact that these under-staffed and overwhelmed agencies had on the people who needed their help. "It [was] not uncommon for as many as fifteen or twenty evacuees to be waiting half a day for an interview," he reported. The Issei (first-generation) men and women were especially challenged by the language barrier, and social service agencies sought to meet their needs by holding English-language classes. The lack of good jobs combined with discriminatory employment barriers and overcrowded living quarters angered those who felt that they had been promised more upon their arrival in Chicago.

WRA community analyst John Edward de Young's report, filed on July 22, 1946, was much more colorful in describing the goings-on in pockets of Japanese American neighborhoods, including the Northside's Yabotown. ("Yabo" means "uncouth" in Japanese.) According to de Young's report, the city and its longtime residents were not prepared for this sudden influx of Japanese Americans. Chicago had a well-established labor history, going back to the 1880s,

Young Nisei men, most of whom grew up in the Boyle Heights neighborhood of Los Angeles, adjust to their new lives as "resettlers" in Chicago, 1944.

yet the WRA had failed to inform groups such as the AFL-CIO about the impending arrival of Japanese Americans and the necessity of providing jobs for them. As the Nisei entered the workforce, sometimes unwittingly as scabs, tensions invariably arose.

It was definitely a rough reentry post-camp, and yet public sentiment did seem to change over time; in some cases the long-term residents didn't just learn to tolerate their new neighbors but actively embraced them. As an example, take the case of the Chicago-area restaurant owner who, because his son had been killed in the Pacific theater of war, objected to the hiring of Japanese Americans by the nearby Curtiss Candy Company (creator of both Baby Ruth and Butterfinger candy bars). The situation got so bad that the WRA effectively stepped in, and within a few years, the Nisei leader of the Chicago Resettlers Committee (CRC) was helping to recruit candy workers directly from camp; in 1944, when wartime employment peaked, three hundred Japanese Americans were hired by Curtiss.

Chicago turned out to be hospitable for many resettlers, but not all Midwest cities were so accommodating. Before ending up in Chicago, Sue Kunitomi, a young, single Nisei who had been a reporter for the *Manzanar Free Press*, went first to Madison, Wisconsin, which she found to be beautiful and idyllic but with only limited occupational and educational opportunities for Japanese Americans. The University of

Left to right: Kenneth Uchida, Frank Oda, and Frank Fukuchi, Chicago, c. 1944. Uchida, who lived in the Maryknoll Catholic Home before the war, and Fukuchi were both incarcerated at Manzanar and arrived in Chicago after the spring of 1943; Oda was incarcerated at the Amache camp in Colorado.

Wisconsin denied her admission, and jobs were few and far between. Another young Nisei, William Hohri, encountered the same situation in the Madison area and ended up working for a time on a farm—not the career he'd hoped to enter into once he left Manzanar. In March 1945, William's father, a Christian minister, was still in camp and making plans to resettle near his son, but because William could not write in Japanese to inform his Issei father that people of Japanese ancestry were not welcome in Madison, William ended up traveling all the way back to Manzanar via train and bus to tell his father not to come. At the sentry gate, William was turned away by Manzanar guards because he didn't have

Right: According to the original caption for this WRA photo, taken by Charles E. Mace in Chicago in August 1942, "Another freedom of considerable importance to the young feminine mind in America is the freedom to shop for and wear pretty clothes."

The YMCA sponsored wholesome mixers and social gatherings like this "All-American Fun Night" for Nisei resettlers, January 1944.

a proper pass to visit the camp, and he ended up going back to Madison without seeing his father. "I cried," William said. "I was just worn out and tired, and slept most of the way back to Wisconsin."

Fortunately, both Sue Kunitomi and William Hohri found more promising opportunities in Chicago. Sue's brother Hideo already lived in the Windy City, and she was able to find work there as a clerk at the Newberry Library. Having come from Manzanar and, before that, the ethnically homogenous neighborhood of Lincoln Heights, just east of downtown Los Angeles, Sue found her new community invigorating, and she says she felt liberated living on her own in an integrated environment. William also moved to Chicago and pursued his education while working full-time. "I was very fortunate to go to the University of Chicago because they had sort of remedial classes," he said, referring to the gaps in his education that resulted from going to high school behind barbed wire.

While Chicago provided a brighter future for these two young Japanese Americans, the freedom afforded others sometimes opened the door to trouble. Although dances and social activities were sponsored by churches and other organizations with the best interests of the youth in mind, some young Nisei, away from the watchful eyes of parents, instead frequented bars and "floated from job to job" with "no sense of responsibility," according to WRA

Sue Kunitomi Embrey at the Newberry Library, Chicago, 1944.

community analyst John Edward de Young. He further reported that Playtime, a bar owned by two Jewish Americans and a Japanese Hawaiian and that catered to Nisei G.I.s during the war, was said to have had white "pick-up girls" working there to encourage customers to spend money on drinks; some were professional prostitutes.

Gambling was also rampant, and in a famous raid of Chicago's South Side Nippon Club in August 1946, forty-five men were arrested—all of Japanese ancestry. (The establishment itself was a legal private club and was back in operation the next day.)

The Chicago Resettlers Committee even produced a juvenile delinquency report, on December 19, 1946. It counted fourteen babies born out of wedlock and noted that requests for abortions were on the rise. More seriously, one Japanese American man was serving a life sentence in a federal penitentiary for being part of a "hold-up gang," while another was rumored to have been a serial rapist. "Some of the spoilage is unfortunately beyond the power of any local agency or program to reclaim," stated the report.

Everything considered, however, Chicago was still viewed as a more welcoming place than Los Angeles immediately following the war, but as months passed, the concentration of Japanese Americans in Chicago gradually diminished, and by mid-1947 most had returned to the West Coast.

Other Midwest destinations also took in former incarcerees, and some of them never left their new towns. This was true of Aiko Hamaguchi Morita, who had worked as a nurse at the Manzanar hospital and as such was a popular subject of photographer Ansel Adams, who visited the camp in 1943. Born in Long Beach, Aiko was living in Gardena with her family when World War II began. Her father, Suyeno, was immediately arrested and taken to an alien internment camp operated by the Department in Justice (DOJ) in Santa Fe, New Mexico, where he lived for a time before eventually joining the family in Manzanar in 1942.[6]

---

6. Immediately after the bombing of Pearl Harbor, the FBI investigated and apprehended aliens and selected citizens for temporary detention. These "enemy" aliens were interned in DOJ camps run by the Immigration and Naturalization Service. The DOJ interned approximately twenty-one thousand aliens and family members of Japanese, German, and Italian descent

On December 8, 1943, Aiko was granted leave to move to Detroit, Michigan, an area that was already roiling with racial tension. Detroit had been home to a large population of Ku Klux Klan members since before the war, and discrimination remained rampant, not just casually but also systemically through local policies governing housing and education. Records show that three thousand Japanese Americans were able to resettle and make some kind of living in Michigan, but it couldn't have been easy, and in some cases their stays were only temporary.

Nurse Aiko Hamaguchi Morita, as photographed by Ansel Adams at Manzanar, 1943.

Aiko's sojourn, as it turned out, was not short-term. In Michigan she married another Nisei, Yoshikazu Morita, who had been studying nursing at the University of California, Berkeley, before he was incarcerated in Heart Mountain Relocation Center. After the war he became a physician and eventually rose to serve as the chairman and chief of nephrology at William Beaumont Hospital in Birmingham, Michigan. He died in 1976, and Aiko spent the rest of her life in Michigan, dying there in 2013 at the age of ninety-four. Her remains were buried in Southern California, near those of her extended family.

---

during the war. There were also WRA-operated citizen isolation camps at Moab, Utah, and Leupp, Arizona, for suspected American-born "troublemakers."

RESETTLEMENT ON THE EAST COAST

Not all resettlers dispersed to the Midwest, and one of the most popular destinations on the East Coast was New York City. In mid-1942, there were approximately two thousand Japanese Americans living in the Big Apple; within four years that number tripled to six thousand. Among those making their way in the city were two members of the remarkable Togasaki family of San Francisco. Of nine children, six sisters went into medicine—three as doctors and three as registered nurses. Before the war, Yoshiye, the third sister, had been the second Nisei accepted as an intern at Los Angeles County General Hospital, considered one of the best medical facilities in the world in the 1930s, and during the war she continued to practice from within the camps. With expertise in communicable diseases, she entered Manzanar early to ensure that incarcerees were properly immunized. After joining the Tule Lake camp medical team, she eventually left California to enter a two-year pediatrics residency at Bellevue Hospital in Midtown Manhattan near the East River.

Her younger sister, Teru, also went to New York City to complete her residency, specializing in tuberculosis. After completing their medical training, the two sisters moved on: Yoshiye became a captain in the U.S. Army and shipped off to Italy to care for war refugees and Italian prisoners of war with the United Nations Relief and Rehabilitation Administration, while Teru decided not to return to her general medical practice in Sacramento and instead opened an office in Honolulu, Hawai'i.

While the Togasaki sisters went to the Big Apple for their short-term medical training, other Japanese Americans made New York their more permanent home. Henry Fukuhara left camp to scout out resettlement possibilities on behalf of his wife, Fujiko, as well as his parents and extended family, all still in Manzanar. After bouncing from Denver to Chicago, Henry arrived in New York City with hopes of discovering the same type of positive opportunities his family had experienced in the nursery business in West Los Angeles immediately before World War II. He stayed in the Sloane House YMCA and visited the War Relocation Authority (WRA) office in the Empire State Building.

After checking out options in New Jersey and Pennsylvania, Henry connected with a city official who had a bankrupt greenhouse operation on his property in Farmingdale, Long Island. Agreeing to be the new manager for the struggling enterprise, Fukuhara sent for his family. They and Japanese American families from another camp attempted to grow carnations, and ten months later, Henry sought to establish his own business. Through money saved from a quick sale of his family's Los Angeles–based nursery, he acquired a greenhouse and two hot houses in Deer Park, in Suffolk County, New York. He and two brothers ran a wholesale flower business specializing in chrysanthemums for more than forty years. Henry, who had prematurely ended his arts education in Los Angeles due to the Great Depression, found creative inspiration and community in New York and began to pursue watercolor painting in his spare time.

Left to right: Henry Fukuhara, his brother Willy, and their father, Ichisuke, prepare flower beds at Calderone Greenhouses in Farmingdale, Long Island, April 1945. Photo by Stone Ishimaru.

Another Nisei, Momo Nagano, graduated from Manzanar High School in 1943 and was recruited by the NJASRC (National Japanese American Student Relocation Council) to attend Wheaton College in Norton, Massachusetts. Her older brother, Daisuke, was already enrolled at Yale University, and Momo's education-oriented parents thought that since Massachusetts bordered Connecticut, Wheaton, an all-girls' college, would be a good fit for their daughter.

Momo was the only non-white American student at Wheaton, and she recalls that when Daisuke first dropped her off at the school late at night and she walked into her dormitory, "every student was standing there, waiting to see what I looked like. [It was] real spooky."[7]

While one of the deans was rumored to have been unhappy about the seventeen-year-old's presence, a cadre of students in her class embraced Momo and her droll humor. One girl especially went out of her way to be nice, Momo remembered. "Not everyone was."

Momo also learned that discrimination often took the form of being misunderstood, of feeling like no one really grasped who you were and what your life was like. One day Momo was sitting in the waiting room of a dentist's office in Norton when someone asked her, "Are you Betty Wong, the laundryman's daughter?" When Momo explained that she was a student at the college, everyone seemed surprised, as a Christian liberal arts college wasn't a place they'd expect to see a teen-aged Asian girl.

Momo also faced challenges her fellow students didn't: as long as the war continued and the exclusion law remained in effect, she had to rejoin her family in Manzanar during summer breaks. "I'd say that I was going to camp; everyone thought I was going to a summer camp," she recalled. She earned her bachelor's degree in history in 1947 and moved back to Los Angeles, where she started a family and became a respected textile artist.

Although their lives ended up being very different, Momo Nagano and Teru and Yoshiye Togasaki followed a trajectory common for many of those who were released to Midwestern or Eastern cities

---

7. Momo Nagano's quotes come from her son Dan Kwong's video production *Momo's Excellent Adventure*.

Momo Nagano *(second from right)* and friends at Wheaton College, Massachusetts, c. 1945.

during the war: before too long, they returned to the West. Even Henry Fukuhara retired in Southern California after a span of several decades. Records show that by mid-1947 the Japanese American population of Chicago—where the highest number of incarcerees went—had dropped dramatically. The mission of Dillon S. Myer and the WRA had failed. They had wanted to eliminate California's Little Tokyos and to disperse Japanese Americans through the general population, yet the community members themselves resisted complete assimilation, and many, in fact, were more inclined to "bunch up" in response to the discrimination they faced in the postwar climate. While some families had, as de Young wrote, "nothing to call them back to the West Coast" and therefore stayed in Chicago, New York, or any number of other cities, others were glad to finally return home and see what they could salvage of their former lives.

SEABROOK FARMS

In 1943 and 1944, while Mary Chiyoko (Yamashita) Nagao worked in Manzanar's garment factory and took care of her twins, Irene and Pauline, her husband, Charles Toshimasa Nagao, was away on furloughs harvesting sugar beets—a vital service while many of the country's farmworkers were serving in the military. In October 1944, Mary attended a recruitment talk by two representatives from Seabrook Farms, Harold Ouchida and Keoru Kamikawa. They had come to Manzanar to extoll the virtues of employment at one of the country's largest processing plants of canned, frozen, and dehydrated vegetables. The factory, located 125 miles south of New York City in Cumberland County, New Jersey, produced the popular Birdseye brand and also supplied food to the U.S. military. Wartime labor shortages meant Seabrook Farms needed more laborers, and with

6—View of Seabrook Farms, Bridgeton, N. J.

Seabrook Farms, owner of the Birdseye brand of "frosted foods," became the leading supplier of frozen, canned, and dehydrated vegetables to the U.S. military during World War II. Postcard, c. 1940.

the promise of affordable housing, free schools for Irene and Pauline, and year-round work, Mary was ready to move three thousand miles to southern New Jersey—and fast. A large group had arrived earlier that year from Poston concentration camp (officially named the Colorado River Relocation Center), and it was rumored that spots remained for only a hundred or so families.

Mary determined to be one of these families, but Charles balked. He wanted to complete his beet harvest contract and was already attuned to the racism they were likely to experience outside of camp. "Life was very difficult there too," he recalled, speaking of his time spent in eastern Oregon and parts of Idaho, which he remembered as rampant with "hatred and discrimination." Restaurants refused to serve Nisei workers, and barbershops would "welcome slitting your throat if you came in to try to get a haircut."

Mary didn't back down, however. She received a permit to leave camp and took the bus to visit Charles in Idaho. "Either you come," she implored him, "or I'm going to take the twins and we're going to go."

The young family left Manzanar together on November 11, 1944, and never again lived on the West Coast. By January 1947, Seabrook Farms—promising "Music while you work –no savings needed – year around employment"—had attracted 2,500 Japanese Americans from the ten concentration camps, including about 450 people from Manzanar alone.

Although Mary may have been lured by the company's "beautiful, enticing brochures" and the promise of moving "out into the free country air," as Charles later reflected, he described their new life in decidedly bleaker terms. "The housing situation reminded us immediately upon arrival as another camp," he remembered, "because we're in those barracks, and everything had to be set up by ourselves. All the beds were still in the crates . . . [and] we had to burn coal—something we [hadn't] done in our lifetime! . . . You had to buy a chunk of ice to refrigerate your [Japanese] foods . . . Well, anyway, so life began—we picked ourselves up, and worked at Seabrook

Above: The Nagao family—Mary, Charles, Pauline *(left)*, and Irene—at Seabrook Farms near Bridgeton, New Jersey, c. 1945, in front of Charles's prized possession, a 1939 Buick he had bought used in 1944.

Below: Pauline and Irene's younger brother, Scott Nagao *(left)*, grew up at Seabrook Farms. Here, Scott, fellow scout Kay Ichinaga *(seated)*, and an unidentified friend work for merit badges by planting trees and performing other acts of public service, 1950.

During the 1940s and '50s, thirty-two ethnicities were represented within Seabrook's workforce, with more than twenty languages spoken around the farm. Japanese American employees at Seabrook represented the largest ethnic group to work for a single U.S. employer at the time. Seabrook Farms employee badges, 1940s and '50s.

Farms, and those of us who had enough ambition and desire to want to advance, we made our way."

For those starting out as ordinary laborers like Charles and Mary, work consisted of twelve-hour days, seven days per week, compensated at fifty-five cents per hour. Charles became a foreman in "raw material receiving" and Mary worked the production line while the twins, and later their younger brother, Scott, attended Seabrook Elementary.

The food-processing giant attracted a multicultural workforce of employees who were willing to tolerate its particular brand of corporate paternalism; quite often the workers were people who had been displaced by war and/or made vulnerable by prejudice and political upheaval. In addition to Japanese Americans, the "global village" became home to Estonians, Jamaicans, Germans, African Americans, and Japanese Peruvians.[8] Japanese Americans continued to be an important part of the Seabrook Farms community for many years, although by 1949 their numbers were down to around 1,200, and by the 1970s there were only 530 Japanese Americans still on the payroll.[9]

---

8. Under pressure from the United States, sixteen Latin American countries interned residents of German, Italian, and Japanese descent; 2,264 Japanese nationals, 80 percent of them residing in Peru, were deported to a DOJ center in Texas, where they were to be exchanged for U.S. citizens held as prisoners of war.

9. Kelli Y. Nakamura, "Seabrook Farms," Densho Encyclopedia, http://encyclopedia.densho.org/Seabrook_Farms/.

RESETTLEMENT IN THE NEAR WEST

Republican governor Ralph Carr of Colorado was the only state governor in the West to publicly oppose the forced removal of an entire ethnic community on constitutional grounds.[10] He also welcomed Japanese Americans to move from military zones on the West Coast into Colorado and warned his constituents in 1942, "If you harm them, you must first harm me."

Buoyed by Carr's support, Japanese Americans began to move into Colorado even before the official exclusion orders were enforced. The family behind a very successful flower growing business with a presence in both Northern and Southern California, the Shinodas, found work on a small farm in Grand Junction, Colorado, in 1942. When the patriarch, Kumaichiro, was impaired by a stroke, his youngest son, Dan, asked that extended family members leave Manzanar to help care for him. Among those making the trek were Hide Shinoda and her two teenaged children, Grace and Larry. After launching an expansive California business, Kumaichiro unfortunately died in exile in December 1944 at age seventy-five.

Second only to Chicago, Colorado's capital city became the most popular destination for Japanese American resettlers. Denver already had a well-established Japanese community, including both a Buddhist temple and a Christian church, not to mention two of the only four Japanese American newspapers to remain in operation during the war: *Rocky Shimpo* and the *Colorado Times*. Into this city in 1944 came eighteen-year-old Rose Hanawa, a recent graduate from Manzanar High School. Her older sister, Machiko, was already in Colorado at the Seton School of Nursing, while two brothers had been released to settle in Ordway, described by Rose as a "very dry and arid" area

---

10. Carr opposed incarcerating Japanese Americans en masse but still agreed to allow the opening of Granada War Relocation Center, located in the far southeastern corner of the state near the Kansas border. Granada, also known as Amache, held a little more than seven thousand Japanese Americans from California. "As a good American, if this is what the war effort requires, Colorado will do its duty," he said. Criticized for his support of Japanese Americans by his political opponent, Carr lost his bid for U.S. Senate that same year.

in the southeastern part of the state. Their oldest brother, Tom, had been drafted into the U.S. Army in April 1941, just months before the bombing of Pearl Harbor.

The costs of Rose's train trip and her first year of tuition at the University of Denver were almost entirely covered by the NJASRC (National Japanese American Student Relocation Council), the consortium of faith-based organizations led by the American Friends Service Committee. Working at the behest of the WRA, the council forged relationships with various government agencies, universities, and philanthropic organizations to make it possible for more than forty-three hundred Nisei to leave their respective camps and continue their higher education at more than six hundred different schools.

Rose lived with a local family and worked as a nanny and housekeeper there to earn her room and board. She was fortunate to have the support of the university, but she still had to deal with the various practicalities of resettlement, not to mention the lingering psychological trauma of her family's incarceration and relocation. While living in Ordway, her mother experienced a "total nervous breakdown," and Rose had to miss one quarter of school to assist in her mother's care. When Machiko graduated from nursing school, she took over. "[My mother] recovered fairly well," Rose recalled, "but she was never the same person again . . . . Having experienced the camp life and all the stresses, it was too much for her."

Manzanar H.S. Class of '44

Rose Hanawa

Rose Hanawa's Manzanar High School graduation photo, 1944.

MAKING A HOME IN TEMPORARY HOUSING

Back in California, Japanese Americans continued to reenter society, and among the many difficulties they faced, one of the most pressing was finding housing. In some areas, such as Detroit and Los Angeles's Little Tokyo, the issue was compounded by the shift in demographics that had occurred when Japanese Americans were relocated into the camps and African Americans from the South arrived to help with the war effort. In Long Beach, Los Angeles County's second biggest city after Los Angeles, the black population had increased tenfold during the war and was up to fifteen thousand in 1945. A majority of the newcomers lived in the Cabrillo Homes project, a block of federal temporary housing that was divided into three tracts. The African American residents accused the management of segregation, claiming they were most often assigned to live in the less-desirable tract, but the Federal Housing Administration denied any wrongdoing.

Cabrillo Homes was the postwar destination of the family of Jeanne Wakatsuki Houston, who would later co-write with her husband, James D. Houston, the seminal Japanese American World War II memoir *Farewell to Manzanar*. Through the AFSC, which had also found the family temporary housing when they were displaced from Los Angeles's Terminal Island in 1942, the Wakatsukis were able to move into a three-bedroom apartment with an inside toilet. "As soon as the front door was closed, Papa went in and flushed it, and when it worked, we all hooted with delight," she wrote in her memoir.

But eventually the charms of Cabrillo Homes wore off, and Jeanne remembers seeing it for what it was. "It looked like a half-finished and under-maintained army base. Long, two-story stucco buildings were set in rows like barracks," she described from the point of view of her teenaged self. The bannisters were peeling, and the lawn was little more than "ragged strips of grass." It didn't feel like home, but it was the only home they had, as their old neighborhood on Terminal Island had been plowed down by the government after all of its residents, including about three thousand Japanese Americans, were evacuated and relocated in February 1942. The fishermen and cannery workers had literally no place to return to after the war.

Not far from Long Beach's Cabrillo Homes was the Truman Boyd Manor, located on the west side of the city near oil fields. This was another temporary housing project created by the U.S. government, this one for defense workers and military personnel. Approximately one thousand bungalows were built on ninety acres of land, and after World War II, its inhabitants were a mix of military tenants and Japanese American families.

In October 1945, Ikuko "Iku" Kato, then almost six years old, traveled with her family from Manzanar in a GMC truck that had apparently been held for her father, Takashi, by former neighbors

American Gold Star Home,
486 TRUMAN BOYD MANOR   LONG BEACH 10, CALIFORNIA

Postcard view of Truman Boyd Manor, a one-thousand-unit housing project built by the Federal Public Housing Authority for military families, c. 1953. Here it is labeled a "Gold Star Home," a name that came about when the American Gold Star Mothers acquired the project in 1953 for parents of fallen World War II soldiers.

in Los Angeles. The family of five crammed into the cab and made their way to Truman Boyd, where they lived in one room of a bungalow they shared with another family. After three months, Takashi found a rental in the nearby suburb of Torrance, and although it was a step up from the shared bungalow, it wasn't exactly a dream home.

The house was on Meyler Street near Harbor General Hospital, on a dirt road with only a few other houses. To Iku's eyes, the property felt big, but the house itself was only one room, with no indoor bathroom. They strung a robe on a clothesline to separate the kitchen from the sleeping quarters, and an outhouse stood away across the field. When it was bathtime, Iku's mother, Shizuko, boiled water in a kettle and poured it into a galvanized aluminum tub. When it was Takashi's turn for a bath, the proud family patriarch had to fold his knees to his chin to fit in the washbasin.

The landlord, another Japanese American, had been miserly and even "nasty" to the Katos. When he realized he could get more money for the property than what they were paying, he harassed the family, going so far as to contaminate their vehicle's gas tank. Life on Meyler Street became a nightmare, and Takashi desperately tried to save money from his gardening route so he could move his wife and children away from the abusive landlord. In 1947 he did, moving the family to a five-acre property in north Torrance, just south of Gardena, which by this time was on its way to becoming a Japanese American enclave.

Takashi and Shizuko Kato inside the nursery they owned and operated in Gardena, c. 1962–63. They relocated their business to Gardena in 1959 when their previous enterprise in Torrance was acquired through eminent domain and demolished to make way for Interstate 405.

BAINBRIDGE ISLAND

Six months after Shigeko Kitamoto and her sister, Fumiko Hayashida, arrived at Manzanar with their young children, they had a visitor from the outside. Felix Narte was looking after the Kitamotos' farm on Bainbridge Island, Washington, where he was part of the small Filipino American community. He had worked for the Kitamoto family for decades and made the nearly one-thousand-mile trip to Manzanar to see them. The visit was covered back home in the local *Bainbridge Island Review*, and the support of both Narte and the paper's editors later eased the Kitamotos' and Hayashidas' return to the island in June 1945, before the war ended.

Walter and Mildred Woodward, editors of the *Bainbridge Island Review*, never ceased to remind their readers that the forced removal of 227 Japanese Americans from their close-knit island community was not only unwarranted and unjust but also unconstitutional. The Woodwards had promoted their young employee Sam Ohtaki to staff correspondent before he was taken to Manzanar (then called the Owens Valley Reception Center), and while he was incarcerated they ran weekly stories written by Sam and other camp correspondents about births, weddings, military inductions, and departures from both Manzanar and, later, Minidoka War Relocation Center, where most Bainbridge Islanders were transferred in February 1943, at their request to join other Japanese Americans from the Seattle area.

After the war, about 140 Japanese Americans returned to Bainbridge Island—just a little more than half the prewar population—and although the community was relatively welcoming and their homes and properties were usually intact, many struggled. Shigeko resumed running the family farm—first restoring her twenty-two acres of raspberry bushes, but later switching to Christmas trees when she had trouble finding berry pickers—and her husband,

Fumiko Hayashida holds her thirteen-month-old daughter, Natalie, while waiting to board a ferry from Bainbridge Island to Seattle, March 30, 1942.

Above: Natalie Hayashida *(left)* was forced to evacuate her Bainbridge Island home as a baby cradled in her mother's arms. At four years of age, she returned to Bainbridge with her family after the exclusion orders were lifted. Here she proudly sports a Brownie uniform alongside her cousin Jane Kitamoto Akita *(center)* and sister Susan Hayashida Fujita, c. 1950.

Felix Norte In Visit To Friends At Manzanar

By SADA OMOTO
Review Staff Correspondent

● MANZANAR, Calif., Wednesday, October 14—Felix Norte, Fletcher Bay Filipino, visited the Frank Kitamoto family here over the weekend.

Mr. Norte manages the Kitamoto farm at Fletcher Bay. Especially glad to see him were the Kitamoto children, to whom the evacuation still is a puzzle.
★ ★ ★ ★ ★

Above: Bainbridge Island Review, October 15, 1942. (Felix's last name is misspelled "Norte" in this article.)

Above: Shigeko Kitamoto and her children on the day of their forced removal from Bainbridge Island, Washington, March 30, 1942. *Front:* Ilohio Narte holding Frank Kitamoto. *Back, left to right:* Jane Kitamoto being held by an unidentified man, Lilly Kitamoto, Shigeko Kitamoto, Frances Kitamoto, and Felix Narte. After the war, the Kitamotos sold an acre of land to Felix for one dollar as thanks for his help.

Frank, opened a small jewelry store in Seattle. (He had worked for Friedlander's Jewelers in Seattle before the war, and upon his release from Minidoka he had spent time in Chicago learning watch repair.) Her sister's family, meanwhile, faced steeper financial hurdles, in part because they grew strawberries, for which profits can be earned only after making investments in the plants themselves, followed by two years of cultivating. In 1950, Fumiko, her husband Saburo, and their three children gave up farming and moved to Seattle, where Saburo worked for Boeing until his retirement.

Shigeko later explained that she *needed* to go back to the Pacific Northwest, and specifically to Bainbridge Island, "where I was born and raised." It was a sentiment no doubt echoed by thousands of others, but unfortunately not everyone was lucky enough to get the chance.

LIFE IN TEMPORARY HOUSING

The Muraoka family, among the last to leave Manzanar, had a housing dilemma. There were the parents, Eddie Shigeo and Hatsuno ("Hattie"), and their eight children, including a newborn, Joyce Sueko, born three weeks earlier. After the boys had released their wartime collection of thousands of marbles into the basketball court near the camp barracks, they boarded a bus, once again unsure of their destination.

They felt an unsettling déjà vu when they arrived at yet another huge camp—this one not of barracks but of trailers and located only five miles from where, three and a half years earlier, they had gathered to take buses to Manzanar. In a surprising twist given that Japanese Americans had been incarcerated because they were considered potential threats to national security, this trailer camp, located at the intersection of Winona Boulevard and Hollywood Way in Burbank, was across the street from an airport used by defense contractor Lockheed. The trailers themselves, a drab military brown, had previously been inhabited by soldiers of the U.S. Army. Between fall of 1945 and spring of 1946, the Winona camp housed between five hundred and six hundred former incarcerees, with each family paying around twenty dollars per month.

Since the Muraoka family was so large, they were assigned to three trailers—one large, with a kitchen and a living room, and two small, with bedrooms. The *Pacific Citizen* newspaper described the living conditions, which were not dissimilar from those the resettlers had just left behind in camp: "Families will live in single rooms of 12 to 20 feet, partitioned from larger frame structure barracks abandoned by the Army some time ago. The FHA supplies an iron cot, mattress and two blankets per person, and the only other household article provided is a heating stove. There is no running water or toilet facilities in the rooms, and the evacuees will be fed from a community kitchen."

These trailers were managed by the Federal Public Housing Administration (FPHA), and the agency's director was no other than

Dillon S. Myer, the same person who had overseen the WRA. The WRA, in fact, had initiated the creation of these trailer parks back in September 1945. At that time, the agency had requested thirty sites for temporary housing within Los Angeles County, but only five were approved. Three of the five were in Burbank, and after many city residents opposed what they called a "mass influx" of Nisei, only two sites were given the green light: the Winona camp, where the Muraokas initially moved in 1945, and one called the Burbank camp, at Magnolia Boulevard and Lomita Street, which accommodated two hundred Japanese Americans. The local WRA official stressed that the Japanese Americans would be in Burbank for only a few months: "These people will move as soon as they can find other homes and jobs."

According to the *New York Times*, four thousand former incarcerees lived in converted army barracks and trailers across Southern California,

The Burbank camp at Magnolia Boulevard and Lomita Street, November 1945.

and in addition to Burbank, housing sites were established in Hawthorne, Inglewood, Santa Monica, Santa Ana, and El Segundo. There were two housing sites in Lomita—one a group of barracks at the Lomita Flight Strip, the other a trailer camp for workers at California Sea Food. Another private company, Kings Farm, had a labor camp in Torrance.

One thing the trailer camp residents all had in common was that they were poor. Before the war, patriarch Eddie Muraoka, for example, had worked as a "haul man" transporting vegetables outside of Gardena, and his growing family had lived in an old farmhouse without any indoor plumbing. After the war, the whole family continued working on farms harvesting crops. "We were dirt poor," said Victor, who at age thirteen was the second oldest of the eight Muraoka children. "We had nothing . . . . Part of the glue that held us together is that we had to work and contribute to the pot. I still remember giving all my money, whatever I earned, to my mom."

An observer, Hank Tsurutani, described the living conditions in the temporary housing parks to Tom Sasaki, a field worker for a government study on resettlement: "The Winona camp is a pitiful place," Hank said. "Nothing but old people and a bunch of kids. It is worse than a relocation center. But they have no place to go."

The camp was a firetrap and a health hazard. There were holes in the communal bathroom floor, and children played near busy streets and rotting trash.[11] The noise from the airport was constant. "After a while we got so used to the planes that if there was no activity, it was almost too quiet," remembered Victor, who became an amateur expert on aircraft through his daily observations.

In spite of the substandard conditions of the park, it was not closed but rather expanded when the other temporary housing sites were shut down. On the eve of its own expiration, the WRA, together with the FPHA, assigned an additional five hundred people to Winona, for a total of one thousand, thus deepening the rift between the WRA and the county. Los Angeles County's superintendent of charities, Arthur J. Will, was beside himself, pointing out the lack of lights,

---

11. Charlotte Brooks, *Alien Neighbors, Foreign Friends: Asian Americans, Housing, and the Transformation of Urban California* (Chicago: University of Chicago Press, 2009).

bathrooms, cooking facilities, and even food. When the residents took it upon themselves to shop at local markets, they were turned away. The WRA, which was officially disbanded by President Truman's Executive Order 9742 on June 25, 1946, was busy closing its doors and responded to the housing crisis by funneling complaints to other agencies. Through no fault of their own, these displaced people, whom the *Los Angeles Times* once called a "maelstrom of problems during the war," continued to be viewed as troublesome even after the war.

However thoroughly the Muraokas had managed to settle in at Winona, they were forced to move again when the trailer park closed in September 1947. They lived for a while in temporary housing in Lomita, then finally resettled in a trailer park at San Fernando Road and Olinda Avenue in Sun Valley (near Burbank), which had been opened specifically to house people who had been displaced when Winona closed. "This last trailer camp was not too nice, with junk trailers and very little class," Victor wrote in his family memoir, *When I Was Your Age* . . . .

Finally, in 1950, the family was able to buy a house of their own. The three-bedroom home, located just half a mile from the trailer park, was their first new house and, best of all, it came complete with a built-in toilet and a bath.

FINDING WORK IN POSTWAR AMERICA

If finding housing was the first major hurdle for resettlers, finding work was a close second. According to one source, one-fifth of the working-age population in the Winona trailers was unemployed,[12] and the inhabitants were offered welfare checks from the county and monetary donations from local Quaker congregations. Victor Muraoka remembers he and his siblings "raised holy hell" at the idea of relying on public or church assistance. They told their mother they did not want to accept charity, and over the next five years they took it upon

---

12. Copeland, "Stay for a Dollar a Day."

themselves to earn extra money harvesting crops when they weren't in school.

In Southern California, some local businesses welcomed Japanese American laborers—the California Sea Food and Kings Farm canneries were among those who employed significant numbers of former incarcerees—but for the most part Japanese Americans resettling in Los Angeles turned to the lawnmower and pick-up truck for their income. An inordinately large number of Japanese American men—22.5 percent of total Issei and 16.6 percent of total Nisei—worked as gardeners in postwar Southern California.[13] Some were new to the practice, while others had been gardeners before the war and stayed in touch with their former customers. One of these veteran gardeners was Shigetoshi Tateishi, a thirty-eight-year-old Kibei Nisei (the term used for Japanese Americans who were born in the United States but raised or educated in Japan). Following the December 1942 chaos at Manzanar when military police fired into a protest, killing two and injuring at least eight, Shigetoshi, who had worked as a block leader in Manzanar, was among those removed. He was one of fifteen men sent to isolation centers in Moab, Utah, and Leupp, Arizona, where they remained for several months while the WRA conducted investigations into the incident. Convinced that Shigetoshi had not been party to the violence in Manzanar, WRA officials then sent him to the concentration camp in Topaz, Utah, before returning him to Manzanar in September 1943. Those months changed him, his son John later recalled. "He became much more quiet and, not moody as much as reflective . . . . It took me a while to really feel comfortable with him back, [to feel] that this actually was my father; . . . he was just a changed man. And I always felt like . . . his spirit was broken. That was how he was through the rest of his life."

Upon leaving Manzanar in 1945, Shigetoshi had told his three sons, "Don't ever forget this place, because you're the ones who are going to have to remember it. If you ever have an opportunity to make this

---

13. Ronald Tadao Tsukushima, "Politics of Maintenance Gardening and the Formation of the Southern California Gardeners' Federation," in *Green Makers: Japanese American Gardeners in Southern California,* by Naomi Hirahara (Los Angeles: Southern California Gardeners' Federation, 2000).

Hiram Ida, who was in Manzanar from June 1942 to March 1944, as featured in "For a Greener Tomorrow," a souvenir booklet for the second annual California Landscape Gardeners Convention, in Long Beach, California, 1958.

right, it's your obligation, not just to the family or to the community but to the country."

Before the war, Shigetoshi worked for several high-profile celebrities (including Marilyn Monroe), and one former client in Bel Air, enraged by the forced removal of Japanese Americans from the West Coast, promised Shigetoshi that his gardening job would be waiting for him when he returned from camp. While Shigetoshi gardened and his wife, Yuriko, worked as a domestic on the same loyal customer's large estate, the couple and their sons lived for a time in the social hall of the West Los Angeles United Methodist Church with about a dozen other families.

Other Japanese Americans entered the landscaping field for the first time after the war. In his interviews with community members, government field worker Tom Sasaki found that many of his subjects mentioned the "good money"—ranging from $250 to $600 a month—that could be earned as a gardener. "But it is hard work," said Bob Kodama, a Nisei staff member of All People's Christian Church, which counted many gardeners among its members. "They begin around six in the morning and work until seven in the evenings," he said. He spoke to Tom Sasaki about one member of the congregation who faced so much discrimination from his coworkers at an aluminum company that he opted to become a gardener instead of enduring the bias. He eventually took a civil service examination and began working for the government, as did many Nisei, especially those who were military veterans.

Beyond gardening, many former incarcerees found success as independent business owners who catered to the Japanese American community, providing housing, particular goods, or certain foods they had been unable to get in camp, like *China-meshi* (Japanese American-style Chinese food). Medical professionals and dentists of Japanese descent also did well, their appointment calendars filled with the names of people who had inadvertently neglected their health care while incarcerated.

But even highly trained professionals faced obstacles as they attempted to resume their careers in the postwar market. Masako

Kuichiro Nishi (right), who operated the expansive Pacific Rose Company in West Los Angeles before World War II, was not able to rebuild his enterprise after his release from Manzanar, but he still participated in local flower shows, like this one in Hollywood Park, March 14, 1954. Standing next to Nishi is his wife, Hiro, and next to her is Mrs. Honma, a teacher of the art of Japanese flower arrangement.

Kusayanagi Miura, for instance, was in the middle of her medical residency at Los Angeles County General Hospital when it was interrupted by the bombing of Pearl Harbor, and she was one of many medical staff who were told by hospital administrators that they would be immediately discharged, although with the option to be reinstated ninety days after the war. Clinging to that promise for more than three years, Masako returned to County General within the ninety-day time period in 1945 and submitted her application for reinstatement.

Recounting the incident in an interview, Masako said she was told, "This is not the propitious time."

"Well, when is the right time?" she asked. "If I don't hear from you, you will hear from my lawyers."

The response from the county supervisor was suddenly more encouraging: "We'll have an opening in six months."

Sure enough, Masako was able to resume her residency without further incident.

••• ••• •••

The early resettlement period for Japanese Americans was full of turmoil and uncertainty. Some entered new regions populated by different ethnic groups and characterized by unfamiliar sensibilities. Others "came home" to the West Coast, yet this home was now a hostel, trailer, or single-family house shared by multiple families. Men with college degrees or who had owned businesses prior to the war took up the maintenance gardening trade to put food on the table. Children went out in the fields to pick or sell vegetables after school to supplement their families' income. While community members banded together to establish a foothold back in American society, Japanese American leaders discovered that they, like Masako Kusayanagi Miura, needed to also be ready to fight, both legally and politically, for a better future.

CHAPTER TWO

WAR IS OVER

Given the new focus on rebuilding their lives, many former incarcerees had no interest in returning to Manzanar anytime soon, if ever. One of those who did, however, was Sangoro Mayeda, an assistant to Reverend Shinjo Nagatomi, who had relocated to the Gardena Buddhist Church in Los Angeles after the war ended. On Memorial Day of 1946, Mayeda returned to Manzanar to perform services for those who were still buried in the cemetery. The dead weren't many: three were older men with no living relatives in the United States, two were premature babies whose parents had been sent to Tule Lake Segregation Center, and one was an unidentified stillborn baby.

As Mayeda recalled in an article in *Rafu Shimpo,* when he returned to the site he discovered it was locked up and inaccessible. A soldier said to him, "Hey, you can't go in there[;] that's U.S. government property!"

"Just a few months before, they had machine guns to keep us in[;] then they put locks and guards to keep us out," he stated.

A larger group was able to make a pilgrimage during the Buddhist summer Obon season later that same year. Two buses took members

Trailer homes in Burbank, California, November 1945.

of the Gardena Buddhist Church, including Shinjo Nagatomi and his friend Jack Iwata, a photographer and devout Buddhist. They gathered around the obelisk, which had been designed by Ryozo Kado, a Catholic. There they chanted and expressed thanks. Joining the group outside the Block 18 mess hall, which had been the last meeting place for Buddhists in Manzanar, was former camp director Ralph P. Merritt. The legendary photographer Toyo Miyatake was also present to capture the historic event in color motion picture film.

The Reverend Nagatomi continued his visits, year after year, into the 1950s, after which his health no longer allowed him to make the journey. The number of people from the Gardena congregation who returned to visit the camp also waned, dropping from one busload in 1946 to a few vehicles the next year, and then finally one single car. Mayeda, who was ordained in 1952 and given the Buddhist name Sentoku, continued the annual pilgrimage to clean the cemetery and to offer sutras to the dead.

Mayeda's son, Mark, who was born in Manzanar on June 14, 1945, accompanied his father on these pilgrimages from age seven to twelve.

Photographer Toyo Miyatake returns to Manzanar with his wife and some of their children, 1952. *Left to right:* Toyo, Hiro, Minnie, and Richard. Archie *(not pictured)* took the photograph.

The trips along the barren two-lane highway between Los Angeles and Manzanar usually started before dawn and ended after sunset. They sometimes had to dig themselves out of the loose soil of the dirt road between the highway and the camp. At the cemetery, they would start by cleaning and repairing the monument, which was pocked with gunshots from hunters and sometimes needed a fresh coat of paint. "After cleaning up, we would have lunch," Mark wrote in a remembrance for this book. "One time we stopped at a restaurant on the road. We sat at a table, but no one would serve us. After that experience we always brought our own food and water. After we ate, my dad would put on his robe and conduct the service."

On one of his early pilgrimages, Sentoku met up with Christian minister Shoichi "Henry" Wakahiro from West Los Angeles, who had been incarcerated in Manzanar with his wife and daughter. Both religious men who had shared the incarceration experience at Manzanar continued annual pilgrimages together until their deaths in the late 1970s. Later activists organized more public pilgrimages, but these lesser-known visits represented the religious community's respect and care for those who had died behind barbed wire. Two of the organizers of the Manzanar Committee, Warren Furutani and Sue Kunitomi Embrey, later wrote of their being humbled by these men. "What we brashly declared as the 'first' pilgrimage [in 1969] was the twenty-fifth one for the two ministers."

POLITICAL GAINS

In the years immediately following the war, and for a long time after, various types of leaders set out to eliminate the last vestiges of anti-Asian legislation and to fight the discrimination that persisted among the general public. They included World War I veterans, artists and photographers, labor activists, and lawyers, both from within and from outside of the Japanese American community.

One of the first major legal battles was in 1946, when two California state senators introduced Proposition 15 to close what they considered loopholes in the Alien Land Laws, which discriminated against Issei—who were still unable to become naturalized citizens—by barring them from purchasing property. In their argument for passage of the referendum, the politicians claimed that Japanese aliens had "indulged in all manner of subterfuges" and resorted to "nefarious schemes and devices" to conceal their status as non-citizens.

One entity opposing the passage of this proposition was the Japanese American Citizens League (JACL), a Nisei-centric organization that had been heavily criticized within the Japanese American community for having allegedly sold out political dissidents during wartime. After the war, the JACL was determined to regain members and represent Japanese Americans on the national stage during the resettlement period, and it actively campaigned against Proposition 15. A leader in this effort was the JACL's Washington, D.C., lobbyist, Mike Masaoka, a polarizing figure who had his share of both admiring supporters and vocal detractors.

Proposition 15 was hotly contested, and the Japanese American community raised $100,000 to fight it. In the end, the ballot measure was defeated 1,143,780 votes to 797,067. According to Ellen Wu in *The Color of Success: Asian Americans and the Origins of the Model Minority* (2013), this was the first anti-Asian referendum to be voted down in the United States. The JACL leadership was elated, with Masaoka stating in the JACL publication *Pacific Citizen*, "The lesson of the vote on Proposition 15 is that the war is over and the people of California will not approve discriminatory and prejudiced treatment of persons of Japanese ancestry."

While the tide was definitely turning, the defeat of Proposition 15 was not the end but rather the beginning of political and legal battles that would consume civil rights leaders and lawyers for decades. One of those individuals was a young Nisei whose legal studies at the University of Southern California had been interrupted by the bombing of Pearl Harbor. Frank Chuman was taken to Manzanar and, at the age of only twenty-four, was recruited as chief administrator of the 250-bed camp hospital. He accepted the challenge and served in that capacity for a year and a half before moving on to Ohio and then Maryland, where he completed his law degree in February 1945.

While at the University of Maryland, Chuman was exposed to
the Old England legal system, also known as "Law Courts," which
included some old and little-known legal procedures. Most notably
among the ones Frank studied was *coram nobis*, literally "before us," a
legal order that allows for the reopening of an earlier judgment based
on new evidence. This procedure would prove to be a game changer,
not only for the Japanese American community but, in fact, for the
nation as a whole.

Years before he would inspire lawyers to employ *coram nobis* to
reverse key court cases related to wartime incarceration, however,
Frank Chuman was shaped by his personal experiences with racism
and discrimination below the Mason-Dixon line. It was there he
determined that he couldn't tacitly accept segregation policies aimed at
the region's black population, and that led naturally into his career as
an attorney fighting for civil rights. "From that moment on, I resolved
that I would not allow differences in race, creed, color, religion, or
gender affect my attitude or behavior toward others," he wrote in his
memoir, *Manzanar and Beyond* (2011).

After passing the Maryland bar exam, he was offered three presti-
gious positions, including an invitation to be on the U.S. government's
legal team to prosecute Japanese war criminals in Tokyo. Chuman
ended up turning them down. The year was 1945: Manzanar was
closing, and he needed to help his parents resettle back in Los Angeles.

Armed with a recommendation letter from Dr. Morris Opler, a
social analyst at Manzanar who later became a Harvard professor,
Chuman was able to get a position with Abraham Lincoln "A. L."
Wirin, a top constitutional lawyer who also served as the JACL's coun-
sel. Wirin's offices were on Spring Street in downtown Los Angeles, a
few blocks away from City Hall, courthouses, and other government
buildings.

According to his memoir, Chuman had not previously been
involved with the JACL and knew little of its activities. Even in his
legal studies his forte had not been constitutional law but courses that
dealt with "tangible facts, not theory." Now he found himself in the
middle of civil rights cases, charged with doing research and writing
parts of legal briefs. He was also dispatched by Wirin to use legal

Frank Chuman (*center*) receives a JACL 1000 Club pin from Tats Kushida as David Yokozeki looks on, c. 1955. The 1000 Club helped fund the JACL's activities.

means to stop the deportation of a number of undocumented Japanese immigrants. Despite his inexperience with the JACL, he was selected in 1946 to be the Los Angeles chapter's first postwar president.

One of Chuman's tasks as a law clerk was to identify Nisei who had renounced their U.S. citizenship during World War II as part of the Renunciation Act of 1944, also sometimes referred to as the Denaturalization Act of 1944 (Public Law 78-405), which allowed Japanese Americans to forfeit their U.S. citizenship during the war. According to Eileen Tamura's *In Defense of Justice: Joseph Kurihara and the Japanese American Struggle for Equality* (2013), 5,725 individuals renounced their citizenship, most of them coming from Tule Lake Segregation Center. While their motivations varied, many had done it as an emotional reaction to their imprisonment, and once the war was over, a number of them realized they wanted their citizenship reinstated.

Of the 5,409 who sought restoration of their U.S. citizenship, most of them were able to do so through ACLU lawyers—notably Wayne Collins and California-born Nisei Tetsujiro "Tex" Nakamura. In 1945 he formed the Tule Lake Legal Defense Committee to pay for legal fees related to renunciation and reinstatement.

KURIHARA AND WAKAYAMA

Joe Kurihara, 22, in his U.S. Army uniform, 1917.

At age forty-seven, Joe Kurihara began to lose his faith in America when he witnessed families being forced from their Terminal Island homes in February 1942. "Here my first doubt of American democracy . . . crept into the far corners of my heart," he recalled, saying it came with a "sting that I could not forget." A Hawaiian-born veteran of World War I, Joe had been away at sea working as a tuna boat navigator when news of Pearl Harbor hit.

Among those ordered to leave Terminal Island were Ernest Kinzo Wakayama and his wife, Toki. Also a veteran of World War I and born in Hawai'i, Ernest was a skilled lawyer who had served as secretary of the Southern California Japanese Fisherman's Association, located on Terminal Island. When the authorities came to evacuate the community, Ernest said he initially wanted to resist, but he changed his mind upon seeing the "fierce-looking faces" of the troops. "To avoid trouble later," he said, he found it "wise to obey."

Terminal Islanders experienced a series of displacements. First, all Issei fishermen had been arrested by February 2, 1942, and were taken to alien internment camps. This was followed later that month by the wholesale expulsion of all residents, including non-Japanese people, from the island. Then, while they were still settling into new living situations, Japanese Americans received exclusion orders that moved them into concentration camps. During this chaotic period, Kurihara attended a meeting in Los Angeles of the Citizens

Federation of Southern California (CFSC), a Nisei organization affiliated with the JACL. He witnessed, aghast, as JACL lobbyist Mike Masaoka urged complete compliance with exclusion orders—even for American citizens and World War I veterans. In that moment, Kurihara resolved to fight the "spineless" members of the JACL leadership "in whatever camp [he] happened to find [them]."

While Kurihara volunteered to go early to Manzanar (then the Owens Valley Reception Center), husband and wife Ernest and Toki Wakayama were imprisoned in Santa Anita Assembly Center, where Ernest soon made it known he would not be silent in the face of such unfair treatment. He protested that using the labor of "prisoners of war" (referring to the incarcerees' work of turning fishing nets into camouflage netting for the U.S. military) violated the terms of the Geneva Convention, and this dissent landed him in the county jail—the first of what would be a series of lockups. But he continued to speak out, including pursuing a writ of habeas corpus filed by the

ACLU on behalf of his wife while they were in Santa Anita, which essentially protested the imprisonment of American citizens without due process of law. This action made a brief splash

Ernest Kinzo Wakayama, impeccably dressed, appears undaunted when arraigned and handcuffed at Santa Anita Assembly Center, June 1942. The original caption that appeared in the *Los Angeles Examiner* belied prevailing attitudes toward his early dissent: "'Troublemakers' at the Santa Anita reception center, these Japanese yesterday were arraigned on charges of conspiring to violate wartime orders." *Front, left to right*: Masaru Kuwada, Ernest Kinzo Wakayama, and Deputy U.S. Marshal George Rossini.

in the pages of Los Angeles newspapers, and it inspired a lasting wariness on the part of WRA officials, even those Ernest would soon encounter at Manzanar. By the time Ernest and Toki arrived at Manzanar in August 1942, Joe Kurihara had already become an outspoken leader of the anti-JACL, anti-administration faction.

Following the December "riot" that had left two inmates dead, the die was cast for both men—as well as for Toki Wakayama, then expecting the couple's first son. One month before Junro Edgar Wakayama, known as Edgar or Ed to his friends and family, was born at Manzanar in March 1943, a three-judge panel in Los Angeles approved the petition for a writ of habeas corpus, but by then it was too late: Ernest already had withdrawn his lawsuit, worn down by the struggle of his new life as an imprisoned American citizen.

As for Kurihara, he would never be the same after his incarceration at Manzanar. Already a survivor of World War I, his disillusionment only deepened after two innocent young men, seventeen-year-old James Ito and twenty-one-year-old Jim Kanagawa, died from shots fired by military police during the Manzanar uprising of December 1942. Kurihara had served as spokesman of the crowd that confronted camp authorities and military police during the incident, and in his later years he continued to denounce the shootings as "murder in the first degree, unpardonable and unforgivable." The deaths of Ito and Kanagawa further sharpened Kurihara's resolve to renounce his U.S. citizenship and expatriate to Japan, leaving the country of his birth forever.

Between 1943 and 1945, the paths of these two World War I veterans would converge and diverge at different places within the network of citizen isolation centers operated by the War Relocation Authority and the Department of Justice's detention camps. While Kurihara was sent to citizen isolation centers for "troublemakers" at Moab and Leupp, in Utah and Arizona, respectively, Wakayama spent time in the Lone Pine jail and later the stockade at Tule Lake, the segregation center where his and Toki's second son, Carl, was born. There he renounced his U.S. citizenship and was sent to the alien internment camp at Santa Fe (from which he saw the Trinity atomic bomb test from afar) before being reunited with his wife and two young sons at the Department of Justice detention center in Crystal City, Texas. He would later compare himself to a "ragged old football" in "the political football game of internment," and he too eventually decided to move to Japan. He considered this the "natural outcome" of having been "branded and declared [a] disloyal citizen" by his own government, and at one point he called special attention to the injustice he had suffered as a veteran, asking U.S. government officials: "Do I have to die twice to show and establish my loyalty? Why? My honorable discharge certificate from the army . . . may be just a scrap of paper, but, to me, it is valuable because I obtained it in exchange for my most precious life!"

From a rain-soaked dock in Seattle, Kurihara boarded the USS *Randall* on November 25, 1945, just a few days after Rev. Nagatomi left Manzanar with the last of the incarcerees. The ocean crossing was turbulent and the steerage accommodations crowded. As another renunciant from Manzanar, Arthur Ogami, recalled: "At high seas it was pretty rough . . . . The bow would come up at least fifty-six feet and go down sixty feet."

Kurihara arrived in his newly adopted country on December 8, 1945, only to discover it had been decimated during the war. The temporary detention center to which he and others were trucked was "stench-ridden" and "filthy," and to add insult to injury, most of his possessions had been stolen. "People were so hungry," he recalled.

Hundreds of people—both repatriates (Japanese citizens) and expatriates (American citizens who renounced their U.S. citizenship)—embark for Japan from Seattle, 1945.

Kurihara soon found work with the U.S. military in Sasebo, an ironic turn of events given that he was now working for the government that had imprisoned him, and from which he had recently severed himself. He was one of more than fourteen hundred renunciants then in Japan, and the United States needed the services of translators and interpreters who could explain cultural subtleties to both sides during its military occupation of postwar Japan. According to historian Eileen Tamura, almost ten thousand Nisei and Kibei-Nisei—both soldiers and civilians—worked at some point for the U.S. military during the occupation.

Arriving in Japan in 1946, Ernest Kinzo Wakayama had planned to reconnect with his family members from Hiroshima, only to discover that they had died in the atomic bomb. At one point he became so depressed that he considered killing himself and his family. But, thinking of his young sons' futures, he hung on and soon settled with relatives in Fukuoka. There he and Toki welcomed a third son, George, into the world.

Kurihara struggled to adjust to his new life in Japan, writing to his old confidante from Tule Lake, sociologist Dorothy Swaine Thomas, that "Japanese [people] in Japan and those abroad can be considered as two different species." He refused to return to the United States unless and until he was "invited" to become a U.S. citizen again. The U.S. government proffered no such invitation, and Kurihara died of a stroke on November 26, 1965, in Japan, almost twenty years to the day that he had left the country of his birth.

Joe Kurihara with his sister Kikuno Nakahara, who visited him in Japan, 1954.

LEGAL VICTORIES AND DEFEATS

While the overwhelming number of the renunciant cases were represented (and won) by San Francisco lawyer Wayne Collins, he wasn't alone in fighting for the rights of the former inmates. The JACL's A. L. Wirin took several key cases to the Supreme Court, and he was the person to whom Issei property owners frequently turned when they found themselves vulnerable to California's pre–World War II Alien Land Laws, which barred immigrants from owning property.

The landmark case was *Oyama v. State of California*, in which the High Court ruled in favor of Wirin's clients, Kajiro Oyama and his Nisei son Fred, who were living in San Diego County. The dispute was over the state's wartime seizure of property Kajiro had bought before the war in the name of his then six-year-old son. With the final ruling on January 19, 1948, the Alien Land Law, which had hung for more than a quarter century like an albatross around the necks of California residents of Japanese descent, as well as other Asian immigrants, was severely weakened. (It was not completely destroyed until *Sei Fuji v. the State of California*, in 1956.)

The year 1948 also saw the final passage of the Japanese American Evacuation Claims Act, a highly compromised effort to award some kind of monetary redress for wartime incarceration. Initiated by the JACL's Mike Masaoka, the proposal went through various versions before being signed into law by President Harry Truman. Restitution

San Diego Journal—Thurs., Aug. 23, 1945—Page 3!

Ready to Appeal Ruling

KAJIRA OYAMA, right, confers with his lawyer, A. L. Wirin, in court yesterday after learning that agricultural land he once operated for his son in the Rancho de la Nacion in Chula Vista will revert in ownership to the state of California.

• • •

Jap to Contest Court Decision Returning Land to California

A. L. Wirin, Los Angeles attorney, today prepared to appeal to the State Supreme Court Superior Judge Joe L. Shell's decision in an Alien Land Law case. . Judge Shell yesterday ruled in

Article on the Oyama case, from the *San Diego Journal*, August 23, 1945.

sought without going through the court system was initially limited to a maximum of $2,500, and those who filed had to verify their claims with prewar receipts, a requirement that was nearly impossible to fulfill given that these were people who had been uprooted from their homes and had lost much of their property—and almost certainly most of their household paperwork. The majority of those who filed claims ended up settling for mere cents on the dollar. Karl and Elaine Black Yoneda, for instance, sought $1,355 to cover the loss of "five cartons of books, pictures, documents and the below Blue Book sale of their Studebaker." After countering with $1,010, the Department of Justice Claims Division later informed the Yonedas that they would only be receiving half that amount, as Elaine, although she had been incarcerated, was not of Japanese descent. "In the end, we received only $460," Karl wrote in his 1983 memoir, *Ganbatte: Sixty-Year Struggle of a Kibei Worker.*

By the late 1960s, the government had distributed a total of only $38 million out of the $132 million in claims. Even Masaoka described the reparations as "pots and pans money." "The victory turned out to

Charles Nagao helps Taki Sakamoto at Seabrook Farms fill out early-evacuation claims paperwork in order to recoup a fraction of her family's monetary losses, 1951.

be only a partial one," he said, "and a costly and vital learning experience in dealing with the feds."

In some unforeseen ways, the Cold War period benefited Japanese Americans in that the U.S. government actively encouraged the embrace of East Asia, in an effort to neutralize what it perceived as the Soviet Union's growing global domination. However, this time of political tension mostly gave rise to politicians and movements that negatively affected the community. Congressman Pat McCarran, a Democrat jurist from Nevada who was an ardent anticommunist, was behind the introduction of two pieces of legislation that captured the attention of Japanese Americans: the McCarran Internal Security Act of 1950 and the McCarran-Walter Act. Although President Truman vetoed both bills, Congress had enough votes to override him and make them law.

McCarran conceived the Internal Security Act of 1950 to institute the registration of communists. Other legislators fought for the act's emergency detention provision, known as Title II, which authorized the government to apprehend any person deemed a threat to national security and to detain him or her without hearing or trial. According to research unearthed by Masami Izumi, a professor at Japan's Doshisha University, the incarceration of Japanese Americans, which had been supported by wartime Supreme Court decisions, served as a model for Title II.

Certain Japanese American leaders were naturally alarmed (as were civil rights activists as a whole) when Title II was passed into law over President Truman's veto. However, the reaction to the passage of 1952's McCarran-Walter Act, which addressed immigration reform, was much more divided. Again as part of a larger strategy to contain communism, the immigration act included provisions to squash subversive activity, and one of the ways it proposed doing that was by giving the government the power to denaturalize a citizen. What the legislation also did, however, was eliminate race as a barrier to citizenship; as a result, Japanese immigrants could finally become

A total of 127 individuals take the oath to become naturalized citizens in a ceremony at the Seabrook Community House auditorium, June 25, 1953. Issei from Manzanar include Haruyo Ikebuchi, Gunsaburo Kono, and Otama and Seitaro Okamoto.

naturalized citizens. But this triumph came at a price, in the form of severe immigration quotas on certain nationalities and ethnicities. For instance, the legislation allowed only 185 immigrants from Japan per year.

Many Issei didn't waste any time and started the naturalization process immediately. Charles Nagao, who had at his wife's urging left Manzanar for work at Seabrook Farms in New Jersey, helped his Issei coworkers become naturalized citizens as soon as the law allowed it, and on June 25, 1953, a total of 127 people, including many former Manzanar prisoners, were sworn in as citizens at the Seabrook Community House auditorium. This was the largest number of Japanese immigrants to become naturalized at one time after the passage of the McCarran-Walter Act.

JAPANESE AMERICANS IN THE U.S. MILITARY

In order that they might secure President Truman's support for reparations through the Evacuation Claims Act, members of the Japanese community sought to draw his attention to their loyal service in the nation's armed forces, not just in World War II but in earlier and later conflicts as well, including the Korean War. One of the most heralded groups was the all-Nisei 100th/442nd Regimental Combat Team, which fought on the European front lines during World War II. The 100th/442nd RCT, which suffered eight hundred casualties, was the most decorated military unit per capita in the U.S. Army. Their heroic rescue of what would come to be known as the Lost Battalion in the Vosges mountains in France came at a terrible cost: the Nisei unit suffered casualties two to three times greater than the 211 who were to be saved.[1]

No less important were the bilingual Nisei who served as translators and interrogators for the Military Intelligence Service (MIS) in the Pacific theater. According to Ellen Wu in *The Color of Success*, the Nisei soldier was an important symbol used by the JACL and other parties invested in validating the patriotism of Japanese Americans.

One notable veteran was Paul Bannai, who was on one of the last buses to arrive in Manzanar from Los Angeles in 1942. Being eager to get out of camp at any cost, that summer the twenty-two-year-old

was granted temporary agricultural leave to harvest sugar beets in Idaho with other young men from Manzanar; in an interview with the California State Archives' State Government Oral History Program he called it "some of the hardest work I had ever done in my life." From Idaho, Bannai went to the Midwest to attend college and then ended up getting a job with a chain of hotels in Des Moines before eventually

Paul Bannai in his U.S. military uniform, c. 1944.

1. *Japanese Eyes, American Heart: Personal Reflections of Hawaii's World War II Nisei Soldiers,* Hawaii Nikkei History Editorial Board (Honolulu: Tendai Educational Foundation, 1988).

volunteering for the 100th/442nd RCT. His ability to speak both English and Japanese got him assigned to the MIS unit, where he was the only Nisei and American in the group translating for Australian forces in Borneo and Indonesia.

He served in Japan and stateside a couple of years after the war and got married on leave in Chicago in April 1946. After his military service, he and his wife, Hideko, returned to Southern California to help resettle their extended family. It was also during this time that he began to feel the need to expose mainstream America to the wartime experiences of Japanese Americans.

As president of the Nisei Veterans Association, he approached RKO Studios and filmmaker Robert Pirosh about producing a movie telling "the story of Manzanar." The project never materialized; as Bannai recalled, the studio's response was, "We cannot make controversial, ethnic movies. It is not going to sell. We are in the movie business to make money."

However, the situation soon changed with the box-office successes of two movies that challenged this theory: the Oscar-winning *Gentlemen's Agreement* (1947), starring Gregory Peck as a journalist who assumes a Jewish identity to expose anti-Semitism, and *Battleground* (1949), featuring Van Johnson as a soldier in the Battle of the Bulge. Now the timing was right.

Pirosh, who won an Oscar for the *Battleground* screenplay, went on to not only write but also make his directorial debut with 1951's *Go for Broke!*, in which Van Johnson plays a bigoted lieutenant assigned to lead the 100th/442nd Regimental Combat Team. Bannai and another MIS veteran who had been in Manzanar, Bruce Kaji, were extras in the movie. Bannai also served as a consultant and was even given a few onscreen lines as a mail clerk and narrator.

The film included other former Manzanar incarcerees as well, including Sanbo Sakaguchi and Jerry Fujikawa, the latter of whom eventually enjoyed a prolific television and film career as a character actor. (In a movie that was released a year later in 1952, Fujikawa played "Man at Fish Market" in *Japanese War Bride*, which depicted an interracial marriage between a Japanese woman and a Korean War veteran.)

Members of the 442nd Infantry whose motto, Go For Broke, means "shoot the works."

M-G-M
presents   **"GO FOR BROKE"**

Copyright © 1962 Metro-Goldwyn-Mayer Inc.   Printed in U.S.A.   1   Property of National Screen Service Corp. Licensed for display only in connection with the exhibition of this picture at your theatre. Must be returned immediately thereafter.   R-62/103

Above: Lobby card for the movie *Go for Broke!,* 1952. *Left to right:* Van Johnson, Lane Nakano, and George Miki.

Below: Actor Jerry Fujikawa's head shot, c. 1965.

Above: Private Ben Hatanaka, on furlough from the U.S. Army, sits under the entrance sign at Manzanar while visiting family members imprisoned there, c. 1942–45.

Military service helped the Nisei in a variety of ways. In his memoir *Jive Bomber*, Bruce Kaji discussed how the GI Bill had helped him pursue a degree in accounting from USC. George Izumi, who had cut biscuits in the mess hall in Manzanar, was sent to baking school by the U.S. Army and was later able to parlay his experience as an army cook into launching a successful bakery business, Grace Pastries. Bannai himself was able to use his accumulated military salary for a down payment on an old three-bedroom house on 51st Street in Los Angeles, into which he moved his parents from their trailer in Long Beach.

Veterans who experienced more frontline combat include Ben Hatanaka, who grew up in a farming family outside Vacaville, near Davis, California. He enlisted in the U.S. Army and was eventually assigned to Company A in the 100th/442nd RCT. After boot camp, he was allowed to take furlough back at the "family home" in Manzanar. In response to his grandmother's request for a photograph, he posed in front of the Manzanar sign at the front gate, never imagining that future generations would be touched by the irony of a soldier visiting family members who had been incarcerated by the government he was serving.

Private Ben Hatanaka in Italy, 1944.

Hatanaka fought in Italy, and he later received a Purple Heart for injuries he sustained there. He was never interviewed about his wartime experiences and did not like to talk about it, according to his daughter, Jill. A family member once attempted to take an oral history, but the experience gave him nightmares and the interview was never completed.

Floyd Tanaka also was not one to discuss the past—including the years he spent as a teenager in Manzanar, his service with the 442nd RCT in the European theater, or the loss of his older brother, a soldier with the same unit, who had been killed in action in France. He did, however, express his admiration for the historical buildings he saw during his military service in Italy, which he said inspired him to study architecture and urban planning at the University of Denver, where he met and married fellow former Manzanar incarceree Rose Hanawa in 1949. Later he was able to pay symbolic tribute to his fallen brother, John Yukio, by designing a monument commemorating the exploits of Nisei soldiers during World War II for the Fairmount Cemetery in Denver, the site of annual Memorial Day services.

A steadfast anti-fascist, Karl Yoneda volunteered to serve in the U.S. military as soon as he could. He left Manzanar in December 1942 to put his Japanese language skills to use for the MIS and to help defeat Axis powers. Dispatched to Burma in early 1944, he was part of a small psychological warfare team that created propaganda aimed at persuading Japanese soldiers to surrender. He later served with the Office of War Information (OWI) in China and India.

Within days of Karl's arrival at Camp Savage Military Intelligence Language School in Minnesota, his wife, Elaine Black Yoneda, and their four-year-old son, Tommy, became caught up in the escalating tensions at Manzanar. Fearing reprisals from pro-Japan factions who opposed Karl's zeal for the war effort, Elaine, a white woman who had voluntarily gone to camp to stay with her husband, sought protection from camp administrators. Along with sixty-three others, Elaine and Tommy were hastily escorted from Manzanar to the CCC camp in Death Valley. She was determined to go to Los Angeles or San Francisco to find a job in the defense industry but was still waiting for Tommy's release papers to come through.

As a white person exempt from exclusion orders, Elaine was free to move at will anywhere within the United States before the war was over, but the same was not true for her four-year-old son. Elaine accepted most of the terms of Tommy's release from WRA custody— namely that she file monthly affidavits "attesting to the fact that Tommy had . . . not been in any fight because of his ancestry [and] had done nothing to endanger national security" and that she "report

Karl Yoneda, as photographed by Dorothea Lange at Manzanar, July 1942.

all address changes" to the headquarters of General John L. DeWitt, who had been a driving force behind the removal and incarceration of Japanese Americans. But a third requirement, that Tommy remain in the custody of a white person at all times, roused her ire. As recorded in Vivian McGuckin Raineri's biography *The Red Angel*, Elaine demanded an explanation. "If Tommy was to spend weekends or what have you with our Chinese, Filipino, or Negro friends, would he be in violation of his right to be in Military Area No. 1?"[2] Frustrated that Elaine always had to "complicate" things, Manzanar's assistant project director Ned Campbell, then visiting the CCC camp, nevertheless

2. Vivian McGuckin Raineri, *The Red Angel: The Life and Times of Elaine Black Yoneda, 1906–1988* (New York: International Publishers, 1991), 224–25.

relented. As long as Elaine fulfilled the first two requirements, she and Tommy could return to the West Coast. They were in Los Angeles by Christmas 1942 and resettled in San Francisco by January 1943.

When Karl returned home from war, he resumed work as a long-shoreman and organizer on the docks of San Francisco and reconnected with friends and comrades in the Communist Party. Although the party had summarily "suspended" its few Japanese American members after the attack on Pearl Harbor—and failed to protest the

Left to right: Elaine Black, Karl, and Tommy Yoneda at Fort Snelling, Minnesota, 1943.

exclusion order in any way—some party members later acknowledged the "blatant racism behind those errors," Karl later recalled, and he remained committed to the labor movement. Even so, he couldn't overlook the racial discrimination he experienced firsthand. In his memoir *Ganbatte*, Karl wrote that he was "appalled at the racism" he encountered while house hunting in San Francisco, even though he was a decorated veteran.

When the family moved to Penngrove, about an hour north of San Francisco, to take up chicken ranching, Tommy's second-grade teacher called Elaine to let her know that he might face difficulty at school. The teacher implied the challenges would stem from Tommy being part Japanese, but Elaine retorted that he was just as likely to encounter it because of his Jewish background, as her own parents were first-generation Russian Jewish immigrants. And indeed, as McCarthy-era prejudices gained momentum, Tommy came home from school one day asking, "Will I have to go into a concentration camp again because my other grandparents came from Russia?"

While Senator Joe McCarthy inflamed public fears of a Soviet-led Communist takeover of American culture and values during the early 1950s, Dr. Fumio Robert "Bob" Naka began working on highly classified Cold War–era technologies, first for the federally funded Lincoln Lab at the Massachusetts Institute of Technology and later at a succession of posts within the private defense industry, the U.S. Air Force, and a little-known government entity called the National Reconnaissance Office, located in Washington, D.C. Bob had been incarcerated at Manzanar with his parents, Kaizo and Shizue Kamegawa Naka. The sixteen-year-old math wiz was studying engineering at UCLA when war broke out. With help from Manzanar teacher Helen Ely Brill and the National Japanese American Student Relocation Council (NJASRC), Bob soon left his parents behind in Manzanar, bound first for undergraduate studies at the University of Missouri and then graduate work at the University of Minnesota and, finally, Harvard. After receiving his doctorate in electron optics from Harvard in 1951, Bob was concerned that his earlier incarceration in Manzanar would be "a big black mark" against his career advancement—after all, hadn't the U.S. government classified him an "untrustworthy American"? His fears soon proved groundless: "I was granted a secret clearance . . . and the first activity I engaged in was to work on the Distant Early Warning Line radar to put stations across the landmass of the North American continent to warn the United States of possible Russian bombers carrying nuclear weapons. That was a very hush-hush project. And it was a fascinating scientific activity. I led a team of . . . two or three people and we invented the first automatic electronic analog signal-detection equipment, which permitted the radar station personnel to be reduced from something like 250 people down to 10 . . . . I subsequently helped design the Ballistic Missile Early Warning System."[3]

Based on his success with radar research for the Distant Early Warning (DEW) Line, Bob was tapped by scientist Edwin Land (inventor of the Polaroid camera and film) in the mid-1950s to tackle the flip side of the same problem, namely reducing the radar profile, or susceptibility to detection, of the United States' top-secret U-2 spy plane when flying over Soviet airspace.[4]

In the 1960s and 1970s, Dr. Naka continued to work on highly classified national security and military programs, including spy satellites for the National Reconnaissance Office and precursors to stealth technologies later used in the B-2 bomber. When a colleague asked Bob about whether he had been "evacuated" during World War II, he readily shared his experiences at Manzanar and during his resettlement in the Midwest and, ultimately, in Massachusetts.

"Gee, Bob," his colleague reflected, "You went from being a distrusted American to one of the most trusted we have. You ran the National Reconnaissance Office. That was a tightly, tightly held secret of the United States government. And you signed papers to the White House with all these tightly held code word classifications on the letter . . . . Only in America could such a transition possibly be allowed."

---

3. Interview with Robert Naka by Paul Watanabe, October 22, 2010, University of Massachusetts, Boston; retrieved from http://openarchives.umb.edu/cdm/compoundobject/collection/p15774coll5/id/65/rec/1.

4. Clayton D. Laurie, "Leaders of the National Reconnaissance Office, 1961–2001" (Washington, D.C.: Office of the Historian, National Reconnaissance Office, May 1, 2002); retrieved on October 7, 2017, from http://www.nro.gov/FOIA/docs/foia-leaders.pdf.

ON THE MOVE

One of the common details in so many stories of incarceration and resettlement is how unstable the living arrangements were for Japanese Americans during the 1940s and on into the 1950s. The remarkable life of Aiko Herzig-Yoshinaga serves as one example of not only how hard it was to be constantly on the move during this time but also how this very movement could sometimes lead to greater opportunities for individuals and/or their children. In 1942, seventeen-year-old Aiko, not wanting to be separated from her Nisei boyfriend, eloped just a few days before Japanese Americans were forced to leave their homes in Southern California. While at Manzanar, she became pregnant, and she counted among her many challenges the fact that there was no attached bathroom in the room she and her husband, Jacob, shared with five of his family members. And that wasn't the only problem. "For the pregnant woman like me, the food was not the best," she said. "I think most of the children who were born in camp like my daughter, at least [during] the first growing-up period, were not really healthy."

Upon hearing that her father, Sanji Yoshinaga, was on his deathbed in a camp in Jerome, Arkansas, Aiko made a request to transfer there from Manzanar. Government authorities told her she could go with her newborn daughter, Gerrie, but her husband had to stay back. Sanji was able to see his granddaughter only once before he succumbed to a weakened heart at sixty-nine years of age on Christmas Eve of 1943.

Aiko's husband eventually joined his wife and daughter in Arkansas but was soon drafted into the U.S. Army. Together with her toddler, Aiko then left Jerome to live with her in-laws, first in Denver and then in her prewar home of Los Angeles. There she studied dictation at a stenotype institute, which also provided temporary job placements. One day she appeared in a potential client's office and had the following interaction:

"Are you the temporary secretary?" a man asked.

Aiko replied that she was.

"Are you Japanese?"

"My parents are from Japan."

"I don't want you. Tell your boss to send me someone else, not Japanese."

"I was shocked," recollected Aiko in an interview for the nonprofit history organization Densho. "I had never had somebody tell me right to my face, because I'm Japanese, 'I'm not going to use you.' . . . I was really devastated."

After her husband returned from military service, the marriage eventually eroded; "the chemistry wasn't right," she said. The couple divorced and Aiko and Gerrie found their way to New York City, where many of the Yoshinagas had resettled. The family had always been extremely artistic, and in spite of their limited income the parents had paid for music and dance lessons for six children, who grew up playing the piano, violin, ukulele, and harmonica. Aiko remembers thinking at the time, "Maybe I'll be the next . . . Betty Grable, Eleanor Powell, or Ann Miller."

While Aiko didn't have that opportunity, her daughter did. Without any formal theater training, Gerrie Miyazaki was cast as an understudy for French Vietnamese actress France Nuyen in the Broadway play *The World of Suzie Wong*, an adaptation of the 1957 novel by Richard Mason about a Chinese woman who works as a prostitute on the streets of Hong Kong. Gerrie acted on Broadway from 1958 to 1960 and starred in the lead role fifty times. In 1960 she played Suzie Wong in a production of the play in Ohio, the same year the movie came out.

As for Aiko, her story was just beginning. Living and working in New York City developed her political consciousness, preparing her to play a pivotal role in civil rights in the future.

POSTWAR ART AND POP CULTURE

Iwao Takamoto was seventeen years old and already a high school graduate when he was forced from his native Los Angeles into Manzanar. The camp's head of education, Dr. Genevieve Carter, recognized that there wasn't much to offer the bright youth in camp and decided to give him full rein to explore his artistic talents. "I have a warehouse full of art supplies for the school and I want you to have access to it any time you want," she told him. Takamoto took her up on the offer and filled a sketchbook with drawings of what life was like in camp.

His talent did not go unnoticed, and before long he had caught the eyes of two fellow Nisei who before the war had been art directors for Hollywood studios. Once they were released from camp, they began to give young Takamoto career advice. "Ultimately, they suggested that perhaps the Walt Disney Studio was the place for me

Iwao Takamoto was photographed by Charles E. Mace "earning while learning" in his job as an apprentice animator at Walt Disney Studios, June 1945.

to be, believing that Walt's animation emporium was fueled by a liberal enough attitude as to hire a person who demonstrated ability," he wrote in his self-titled memoir.

When he returned to the West Coast in spring of 1945, Takamoto followed his elders' advice and cold-called the Disney studio in Burbank. He asked to apply for a job in the animation department and was told to come in with his portfolio, which he then hastily assembled using two pads of paper from a five-and-dime store. Traveling two hours to his interview on a streetcar from his Boyle Heights hostel, Takamoto wasn't terribly optimistic, but, to his shock and delight, he was hired by Disney in May 1945 as an "inbetweener"—an entry-level animator who draws the action "in between" defined poses. His first piece of animation was of Donald Duck running up a hill.

Takamoto's groundbreaking employment was heralded in a portrait taken in June 1945 by WRA photographer Charles E. Mace, the caption of which described Disney's recent hire as "earning while learning." (It also mentioned that Takamoto's father, mother, and two siblings were all still imprisoned in Manzanar.) Takamoto would go on to be a mover and shaker in the animation industry, most memorably as the creator of the character Scooby-Doo, the winsome dog who became the star of a popular cartoon for Hanna-Barbera.

Another young Nisei from Manzanar who made his mark on American pop culture was Larry Shinoda. Five years younger than Takamoto, Shinoda also revealed his artistic talent while using the ad hoc assortment of materials available in camp. During the early months of Manzanar, he used discarded shipping crates for toilets to build reclining chairs. His sister, Grace Shinoda Nakamura, recalled "The word spread like wildfire, and I swear, ten thousand people in the camp came to sit on those chairs."

From Manzanar, Larry, Grace, and their mother went to Grand Junction, Colorado, before returning to Southern California. Larry went to Pasadena City College and then, after serving in the Korean War, began attending classes at the Art Center School of Design, which was then located in Los Angeles. His experience was

Larry Shinoda airbrushes a full-scale car design elevation at General Motors, c. 1960.

disappointing, and the school eventually kicked him out. "I didn't fit in there; my ideas and desires weren't consistent with their expectations, so I was construed as a malcontent, which, in truth, I was," he said in a 1997 interview with *Vette* magazine.

But Shinoda's aborted design education didn't keep him from succeeding in car design—or from finding an outlet for his love of cars in Southern California's postwar hotrod scene. He went on to work at General Motors and is credited with his work on the Corvette Sting Ray, the Z-28 Camaro, and the Boss 302 Mustang.

Two noted Issei artists with established prewar careers continued to produce work in the United States after World War II, although time and experience had changed their perspectives and opportunities. Ryozo Kado, a nurseryman and stone craftsman, had converted to Christianity while in his teens in Japan and joined the Catholic Church in 1929 after producing his first rock grotto for a church in California. At the outbreak of World War II, he had just completed a cloister in Santa Paula for Estelle Doheny, widow of Standard Oil

WIZARD with ROCKS

By FRANK J. TAYLOR

How an architect of nature uses pebbles and boulders to transform bare ground into magic gardens.

Seventy-year-old rock-garden designer Ryozo Fuso Kado. Behind him is the ingenious miniature volcano he erected to serve as a back-yard incinerator for a California church.

Mrs. Kado and her grandchildren in the yard of her Los Angeles home. Her husband says, "Twice as many flowers will grow in a well-planned rock garden as in a flat one."

Left: The shrine and rock garden of Los Angeles' Holy Cross Cemetery. On the grounds are an array of gardens, a 400-foot rock wall, a waterfall and a 30-foot grotto.

Saturday Evening Post feature on Ryozo Kado, the "Wizard with Rocks," August 5, 1961.

tycoon Edward Doheny, and was in the middle of designing a personal Lourdes grotto for the home of the stars of the *Fibber McGee and Molly* radio show.

Although Kado and his family would be in camp for only sixteen months before moving to the New York headquarters of the Maryknoll Catholic order, he left behind a prodigious amount of landscape work in the Owens Valley. "Kado was responsible for most of the iconic features at Manzanar," wrote Ronald Beckwith of the National Park Service. "Faux wood was Kado's hallmark, and he incorporated faux wood features in the design of the sentry buildings and cemetery monument. He is responsible, probably more than any other individual, for the appearance of the camp today." Kado also had created the camp's entrance rock garden and sign.

Kado eventually returned to Los Angeles, dedicating himself to the creation of church grottos instead of private projects, which he felt were "too fleeting." "What I do for the church is forever, so I put my heart and soul into it," he told the *Saturday Evening Post* in 1961. In such places as the Holy Cross Cemetery in Culver City, he integrated techniques learned from his Issei mentor and father-in-law, Chotaro Nishimura, and he even took inspiration from Manzanar, recreating the serpentine rocks there to simulate natural grottos in France and Portugal.

Another iconic body of work to come out of Manzanar were Toyo Miyatake's photographs taken from inside camp while he was incarcerated there. "Miyatake employed his photographic skills to document the hardships and indignities of camp life," explained photo scholar Dennis Reed, who also noted that Miyatake initially had camera equipment at hand only because he had smuggled it in.

Future animator Iwao Takamoto had crossed paths with Miyatake in camp and remembered him as a "fun individual" who had the "same personal flair as Sessue Hayakawa," a popular Hollywood silent film star. Miyatake was known for wearing his signature beret, and Takamoto recalled that the cosmopolitan photographer pronounced France's capital city the authentic French way: "Paree."

Miyatake had been a critically acclaimed photographer in the pictorialist school of expression before the war, as well as Little Tokyo's community photographer. He reopened his photo studio in Los Angeles after his release from Manzanar. In addition to doing freelance work for the *Rafu Shimpo* newspaper in Los Angeles, he continued to take portraits of families, community members, and celebrities. One thing that he couldn't restore, however, was the active community of fellow photographers to which he had belonged before incarceration. A member of several photography clubs, Miyatake had close artistic relationships with photographer Edward Weston and dancer Michio Ito, but by the time the war was over, these partnerships had lost traction in the larger art community. "While [Japanese American photographers] demonstrated a remarkable resilience in rebuilding their lives, the bitter experience of incarceration, their advancing age, and an art world no longer interested in their photographs limited their artistic futures," wrote Reed. "The community of photographers that was so active before the war never reemerged, and the few individual photographs that they produced never equaled the adventurous art that they had created before World War II."

Toyo Miyatake with the box camera he used at Manzanar, 1978.

LOVE AND POLITICS

After a rough start in Madison, Wisconsin, Sue Kunitomi had found her place in Chicago, working at the Newberry Library and living in an integrated neighborhood that made her feel her world was always expanding. She wanted to stay, but her widowed mother called her back home to Los Angeles, and so she reluctantly left the Midwest in 1948. When she arrived in California, she was shocked to see how her family was living in a house in the back of a main one: "There was no running water, just a cold faucet outside. And no bathroom." Sue's family could only use the bathroom or shower when the family in the front house was awake.

It was obvious that the home was not up to code, so Sue went looking for a new place for her family to live. After being turned away by a number of real estate agents because she was Japanese, she finally found a house to rent on Crocker Street near Skid Row and Little Tokyo, and she secured a job with the Los Angeles County Health Department.

While her family's life was stabilizing, Sue also pursued her goal of becoming more engaged in politics. She responded to an advertisement in the *Rafu Shimpo* about a meeting of a group called "Nisei for Wallace," which supported the 1948 presidential candidacy of the Progressive Party's Henry Wallace, who had served as vice president under Franklin D. Roosevelt.

According to Ellen Wu's *Color of Success*, there were a few hundred members of Nisei for Wallace in Los Angeles, San Francisco, Chicago, and New York, and together they lobbied for Wallace's platform, which included immediate statehood for Hawai'i; increased compensation for losses suffered by Japanese Americans due to wartime incarceration; and the naturalization of Issei. Wallace was soundly beaten in the election, failing to gain even one-third of the hoped-for target of four million votes, and Nisei for Wallace then morphed into the Nisei Progressives, which locally protested the eviction of Japanese

American and black residents in Little Tokyo to make way for a new
police headquarters.

The Nisei Progressives also spoke out against the McCarran-Walter
Act of 1952, flatly rejecting the bill that sought to give the government
the power to denaturalize citizens. Whereas the JACL had helped
negotiate provisions of the bill, the Nisei Progressives went so far as
to lobby President Truman to veto the legislation based on the harsh
immigration quotas it imposed on "undesirables" from nations in the
Asian Pacific, Caribbean, and eastern and southern European regions.
The president did veto the bill, but Congress overrode his veto and it
became law that year.

Sue became the secretary of the Nisei Progressives, which included
non-Japanese American members, and at one of its social gatherings
she met a motorcycle-riding man named Cliff Barkley, who became
her boyfriend, much to the chagrin of Sue's mother, Komika. At

Sue Kunitomi Embrey (*right*) and other Nisei for Wallace members demonstrate a
clear set of principles, 1948.

another political event, Sue met another white activist, and their first date was to attend the Nisei Week Japanese Festival in Little Tokyo, after which many other dates followed. Sue was careful not to bring her new beau, Garland Embrey, home to be exposed to Komika's watchful gaze and judgment, but according to their respective oral histories, Garland insisted on meeting his girlfriend's mother. The meeting did not go well.

Komika, a Japanese immigrant, had limited English language fluency but was able to get her message across: "You go home! I no like you."

Garland maintained his ground: "We should talk this over, Mrs. Kunitomi."

His directness overwhelmed Komika, who apparently ran to find refuge in her bedroom. Soon after, Sue had a heated exchange with her mother and moved out. "I'm going to leave and I'm not coming back," she recalled saying.

She stayed a week in the home of a female elevator operator at her workplace before getting married to Garland in 1950, in a church in Los Angeles. At that time, only 11 percent of Japanese Americans in Los Angeles County married non-Japanese Americans, according to social scientist Harry Kitano.

It took an anniversary memorial service for Sue's late father to reunite the newlyweds with Komika. The Embreys sat in the back of the Buddhist temple but were pushed by Komika's best friend to join the family at the front to offer incense. The friend later revealed to Sue, "I told your mother that things are changing . . . She shouldn't be so old-fashioned."

With the birth of Sue and Garland's first child, Gary, in 1955, the family was at last fully reconciled. The couple went on to have another son, Bruce, and continued living and working in Southern California. Sue enrolled part-time at California State University and eventually earned a master's degree in education from USC, after which she became an educator.

Sue Kunitomi Embrey holding baby son Bruce, c. 1958.

GETTING AN EDUCATION

In the 1950s, a new generation of Nisei was growing up outside the camps and being educated—both academically and socially—in how to pursue the American dream. When the Reverend Shinjo Nagatomi and his family first arrived in Gardena in 1945, there were not many students of color attending elementary school with his middle daughter (now known as Shirley), but she nevertheless had a generally positive experience there. "People were pretty nice," she remembered. "It was mostly a white community. But I never felt any prejudice."

That was not the case for Roy Kato while he was living with his parents and two siblings in temporary housing in Long Beach. Roy, the older brother of Iku Kato Kiriyama, recalled being attacked by classmates who had lost family members in the Pacific during World

War II. From the time he entered second grade in Long Beach to the family's move to Torrance, Roy was beaten at school every day. "I did not know what was going on, never having been in a fight before. After a few months, we moved to Torrance, and the process started all over again," he wrote. Then one day, the toughest boy in school, Raul Chavez, stepped in. "[He] decided he liked me, and it all stopped."

Iku's classmates in Torrance were also primarily white, but she reunited with Nisei friends on weekends, attending Japanese language school and church at Rev. Nagatomi's Buddhist temple in Gardena. Iku thrived in school, in part due to the encouragement and tutoring of her teachers, and she progressed from speaking no English as a five-year-old in Manzanar to writing school plays and even radio shows. She also made strides socially; when she began high school she and another Nisei friend, Hatsuko Mary Higuchi, decided that they "didn't want to be bumps on a log. We wanted to participate in school activities."

Iku began running for student government and was undeterred by a series of losses during her freshman year. In sophomore year, she went up against a very popular classmate for class secretary, and although even her teacher wasn't optimistic, she proved him wrong and won. "This means you can never say die," he told her.

When the Kato family escaped their abusive landlord and settled into a home on five acres just south of Gardena, Iku felt the difference. "Gardena was more hospitable as a city," she said. "Torrance was *inaka*, very country with fields. With Japanese [people], they really gravitated toward areas where there would be other Japanese."

Indeed, according to academician Hillary Jenks, Gardena was becoming known as "the ultimate Japanese American suburb"; the population of the ethnic group grew in the area from 741 in 1950 to 4,373 in ten years. MIS veteran Bruce Kaji, who had since become an accountant, had moved with his wife, Frances, to Gardena, where a number of Japan-based companies, including Toyota, were headquartered. Nearby aerospace companies prompted the growth of tract-home developments in the city. In the mid-1950s, Paul Bannai, then a manager of a flower-growing cooperative, attempted to buy one of these homes, only to be denied at first because of his Japanese ancestry.

SEATED (Left to right), Carol Isabelle, treasurer; Ikuko Kato, secretary; Diane Trimiew
Student Court representative; Barbara Hester, vice president.
STANDING: (Left to right), Mr. Stuart, advisor; Bob Walker, Boys' League representa-
tive. NOT PICTURED: Midge Simons, Girls' League representative; Leonard Kissel, Boys'
Court representative.

Iku Kato Kiriyama was the sophomore class secretary at Torrance High School, 1955.

Bypassing the realtor, he went directly to the builder, who was only too happy to sell to the well-respected businessman. Thus began a new career for Bannai: licensed real estate agent specializing in the Japanese American market in Los Angeles's South Bay.

To accommodate the growing population in the Gardena-Torrance area, a new high school, North, was established in 1955, and ambitious Iku found herself in a position to create new traditions there. Other Nisei classmates were also energized and ran for various student government offices. "They had not done that before," she said. "In politics, when there's no incumbent, people want to run for office. It opened it up for them. They would never have done that if North High hadn't been built."

In her senior year, Iku became student body president. She was the second female and first Asian student to have that position. At her former high school, Torrance High, the student body president was usually white and male.

Around this same time, another high school student, Jeanne Wakatsuki, was also finding success in her social scene in Long Beach. "My brothers encouraged me to run for school office, to try out for majorette and song leader, and to run for Queen of various festivities. They were proud that I was breaking social barriers still closed to them," she later wrote in an essay.[5]

Like Iku, Jeanne benefited from being in a new school, and she soon caught the attention of the newspaper staff of her newly established junior high. Instead of writing about her experiences at Manzanar, however, the teenager wrote about a happy prewar memory: going grunion hunting in Ocean Park with her family. "We cooked and ate them there on the beach, the bright moon and bonfire turning night into twilight, while a balmy Southern California breeze cooled the summer air," she wrote.

With such an evocative essay, Jeanne was selected for the journalism class, and she eventually became editor in chief of the school newspaper, *Chatterbox.*

An English teacher also encouraged her to become a writer. The teacher "planted the seed, but it didn't really sprout for many years," wrote Jeanne, who as a young girl came to worry that the fantasy of being "Brenda Starr, Reporter" from the popular comic strip was just that—a fantasy—for a young Nisei woman in the 1950s.

Jeanne eventually did become a writer, and she did eventually write about her time as a young girl in a concentration camp. Her 1973 book *Farewell to Manzanar: A True Story of Japanese American Experience During and After World War II Internment*, which she coauthored with her husband James D. Houston, is now required reading in many schools and has been adapted into a television movie and a stage play. The story is particularly moving as it is told from the point of view of

---

5. This essay appeared in an unusual two-sided booklet produced by Capra Press in 1985. One side featured the byline and portrait of James D. Houston and was titled "One Can Think About Life After the Fish Is in the Canoe," while the other side featured the byline and portrait of his wife, Jeanne Wakatsuki Houston, and was titled "Beyond Manzanar: Views of Asian-American Womanhood."

MAJORETTES—Left to Right: Bev Tischofer, Carolyn Buffalo, Shirley Kramer, Jeanne Wakatsuki, Pat Johnson, Myrna Bucher, Darolle Frush, Joan Warner.

Their Twirling Batons and Lively Step

Jeanne Wakatsuki Houston *(fourth from left)* as a majorette at Long Beach Polytechnic High School, 1951.

Jeanne as a child. She was only seven years old when her family was taken from their Terminal Island home to Manzanar, where they lived until 1945.

John Tateishi, the youngest of four boys, was not even six years old when his family was released from camp. Having grown up inside Manzanar, he first equated America as being the land *outside* of the barbed wire, a place that was dangerous and uninviting. Later, and partly through patriotic songs and movies, he began to revise his impression of America, thinking of it as perhaps a welcoming place where he might someday feel at home.

Adjusting to life in West Los Angeles during the resettlement period, Tateishi quickly became aware that his naive view did not hold up to the reality. He and his brothers were often targets of hostility because of their Japanese ancestry, and the only thing his parents and other Japanese American adults did in response was mutter, *"Gaman"*—don't complain and let's get on with it. Talk of camp was usually taboo except for when he met other Nisei or Sansei boys with the shared experience. Then, the question undoubtedly would arise: "What camp were you in?"

"We created this sort of pecking order, a hierarchy of the really cool camps," he explained. "Manzanar, in our view, stood at the top because it was kind of a tough place. We had a riot; all kinds of things happened at Manzanar."

Over time, their stories became exaggerated and funny, as a way to add entertainment value. They boasted about jumping over a creek that was actually too wide to be crossed that way, or they claimed to have tried burning down a guard tower, when in truth they had only set fire to some minor object.

"What was always interesting to me . . . [was] that, at a certain point, we stopped talking," Tateishi recalled. "We talked about all the fun and funny things that happened, and once that's gone, then there's that other part of the experience. Invariably, we would fall silent."

The shame of what had happened to them during World War II burned inside John Tateishi and many others. Like their parents, John and his brothers could not speak of it. And yet there were so many questions that demanded answers. Why had they been locked up by their own government in the first place? Had they done something wrong? And if they hadn't, shouldn't the government officially admit that they had made a mistake?

CHAPTER THREE

TAKINGASTAND

It wasn't until the 1960s, in the stacks of a library at the University of California, Berkeley, that college student Alan Takeshi Nishio accidentally discovered the truth about his birthplace. He knew he had been born in Manzanar, but he had always assumed it was a farm labor camp in Northern California. The paper he found on campus identified Manzanar in quite a different way: as one of ten detention camps that held Japanese Americans during World War II.

His interest piqued, he tried to discuss his birthplace with his family when he was home in Southern California during an academic break. He was met only with silence. His father, a gardener in the Venice area, didn't want to share any details, and neither did his mother. Just as John Tateishi had found it difficult to give voice to his conflicting feelings about Manzanar as a young boy, so did many older Japanese Americans.

Writer Jeanne Wakatsuki Houston had herself been silent for decades, keeping her wartime experiences a secret from her children and even her husband. It was only at the prompting of her nephew, Gary Nishikawa, that Jeanne began to reexamine their family's

Sue Kunitomi Embrey at an early Manzanar pilgrimage, c. 1970.

collective past. Gary was one of Jeanne's seven nephews and nieces who had been born in Manzanar, and he, like Alan Nishio, was a UC Berkeley student on a search to find out more. Gary visited his Aunt Jeanne with hopes of getting greater clarity about the family's history.

"Didn't you ask your mother and your father?" Jeanne asked.

"Yeah, but they won't talk about it," Gary replied. "They change the subject. It's as if I'm doing something wrong by broaching the subject."

Jeanne attempted to answer her nephew's inquiry, but beyond the same stories of windstorms, lousy food, and playing baseball, she was not forthcoming with details.

"Auntie, this is really weird," he observed. "You're talking like being in a prison . . . was nothing. I mean, how did you feel about that?"

"And for one moment," Jeanne later said in an interview for the Japanese American National Museum, "I allowed myself to feel. No one ever asked me how I felt about that incident." She recalls that she began to cry, even to the point of becoming hysterical. Her nephew watched quietly, stupefied.

"I didn't know what was happening," she said later. "I thought I was having a nervous breakdown."

In spite of her reaction, Jeanne was thereafter resolved to leave behind personal stories of camp for her family's next generation. And yet every time she attempted to write something, she broke down in tears.

"I'm having a tough time with this project," she finally told her husband, the acclaimed novelist James D. Houston.

"What project?"

"I'm trying to write this memoir about my family in camp."

At this point the couple had known each other for twenty years and had been married for fifteen. But Jeanne had never revealed the painful truth of what had happened to her family and the eleven thousand others in Manzanar.

James was stunned by Jeanne's revelation. "This is not something just for your family," he declared. "This is a story that every American should know about. Let me help you write it to get it down."

Above: One-year-old Alan Nishio, now a healthy baby in Los Angeles after recovering from medical problems at birth, c. 1946.

Left: Kiyoshi Nishio, Alan Nishio's father, before he lost his grocery store business, c. 1935.

Alan also discovered his family's truth. Born on August 9, 1945, one of the last babies to be delivered in Manzanar, Alan didn't have an easy start and was taken to the hospital in Lone Pine because his mother was unable to produce milk easily. More struggles awaited the Nishio family when the camp was closed down. His parents, who had lost their grocery store business in Los Angeles before the war, had no place to take their newborn baby and his older sister. At first they lived with family friends in Inglewood, near the Los Angeles International Airport, before finally moving out on their own to Mar Vista. To scratch out a living, Alan's father, Kiyoshi, resorted to becoming a gardener, a profession he never embraced. Alan remembers watching him occasionally visit stores for sale, but there was never enough money to restart another venture.

Alan attended UC Berkeley from September 1964 to December 1966, at the height of the Free Speech Movement, which had flared up in response to the university administration's crackdown on political activities on campus. In high school, Alan had contemplated going to a Christian seminary or serving in the Peace Corps, but now facing picket lines at Berkeley, he could not, in his words, "be neutral," and he had to take a stand. He majored in political science and was soon on his way to becoming an activist.

Many others fulfilled their commitments to social justice during this time, and not just within their own communities. The image of the Shonien orphans waving goodbye to him from behind barbed wire had not left Jack Takayanagi's memory, and he departed camp with an even stronger commitment to helping others. From Manzanar he went on to receive his bachelor's degree from Drake University in Iowa and then earned a Master of Divinity at Colgate Rochester Divinity School in New York City. In August 1963, as an ordained minister, he participated in the civil rights movement's March on Washington—at the time the largest demonstration the capital had seen—and was forever transformed by Dr. Martin Luther King, Jr.'s "I Have a Dream" speech. Two years later, he joined Cesar Chavez in Delano, California, to protest the mistreatment of migrant farmworkers, most of whom were Filipino.

The anti–Vietnam War movement also inspired many Japanese Americans to reexamine what had happened to their families and community during World War II. In this new conflict, the "enemy" again had faces like theirs, and activists protested what they considered to be U.S. imperialist actions against Asia and Asian people during the twentieth century. Title II of the Internal Security Act of 1950, which effectively gave the federal government the power to pre-emptively detain citizens during times of emergency, was still on the books, too, and the world seemed volatile and uncertain. It was time to revisit Manzanar again.

At the end of December 1969, approximately 150 people, mostly young, made their way to Manzanar in buses and private sedans. To protect themselves against the biting winter wind, they came wearing knit beanies, scarves, wool jackets, and thick sweaters. Loosely coordinated by the Organization of Southland Asian American Organizations (OSAAO), this was the first public event to commemorate the significance of Manzanar.

The Reverend Sentoku Mayeda of the Gardena Buddhist Church was in attendance as usual to deliver sutras in front of the obelisk. Others cleaned the cemetery, while Bob Nakamura, a professional photographer who had been only four years old when he and his family were incarcerated in Manzanar, snapped pictures in the spirit of "serving the people." His stunning portraits set against the searing landscape of the Sierra Nevada were featured as a centerfold in the

Centerfold of Bob Nakamura's photographs of the 1969 Manzanar pilgrimage in the January 1970 issue of *Gidra*, an independent publication founded by a group of UCLA students in April 1969. Their mission statement read, in part, "Truth is not always pretty, not in this world. We try hard to keep from hearing about the feelings, concerns, and problems of fellow human beings when it disturbs us, when it makes us feel uneasy . . . . The honest expression of feeling or opinion, be it profound or profane, innocuous or insulting, from wretched or well-off—that is GIDRA."

January 1970 issue of *Gidra* magazine, a beacon for progressive Asian American ideas.

In attendance were two seminal figures from two different generations: Warren Furutani, the son of Manzanar incarcerees who had lived on Terminal Island before World War II, and Sue Kunitomi Embrey, a member of the Nisei Progressives. The two became co-chairs of the Manzanar Committee, borne from this inaugural winter pilgrimage. Two years later, the pilgrimage became an annual event, occurring every year in the month of April.

"For a majority of the people, participating in the pilgrimage has been a way for them to confront the past, and to strengthen a sense of community . . . . [It is also a way] of third- and fourth-generation Japanese Americans gaining information which they have not been getting from their parents," Embrey later explained.

From that point on, Embrey stood on the front lines of preserving Manzanar as a historical site in order to safeguard the nation's memory and to prick its conscience. Flanked by her longtime collaborator, Rose Ochi, an attorney who had been in Arkansas's Rohwer concentration camp as a young child, Embrey steadfastly advocated for the preservation of Manzanar.

The committee's early goal was to have Manzanar designated as a state historic site. Joined by the JACL, they won approval for landmark status in late 1971 from the California State Department of Parks and Recreation. What followed was a heated debate over the language that would be engraved on the site's identifying bronze plaque. The Manzanar Committee and the JACL advocated for the use of "concentration camp," a term that many Owens Valley residents found especially objectionable; they also opposed use of the words "hysteria" and "greed" to describe the factors that contributed to the round-up of Japanese Americans during World War II. Facing pushback from state officials, Embrey and her fellow committee members mobilized the Japanese American community to write letters insisting that the designated plaque have "concrete acknowledgement of the injustice committed by our government."

After tense negotiations, a compromise was reached. The state would provide the language for the first paragraph, while the

Above: Manzanar pilgrimage, December 1969. Sue Kunitomi Embrey is standing just right of center, hands held below her chin.

Below: Manzanar pilgrimage, December 1969.

Manzanar Committee and the JACL would draft the wording for the second. The third paragraph would be a result of give and take on both sides. The plaque, installed in April 1973, says the following:

> *In the early part of World War II, 110,000 persons of Japanese ancestry were interned in relocation centers by Executive Order No. 9066, issued on February 19, 1942.*
>
> *Manzanar, the first of ten such concentration camps, was bounded by barbed wire and guard towers, confining 10,000 persons, the majority being American citizens.*
>
> *May the injustices and humiliation suffered here as a result of hysteria, racism and economic exploitation never emerge again.*

Historic preservation was seen as a way to provide a real, visceral experience to outsiders who may have little knowledge about what had transpired during World War II, but it also inspired activism from within the community. One dedicated advocate was Shi Nomura, a former gardener who now had a fish market and grocery store in northwestern Orange County. He was married to the Songbird

The California State Historical Landmark plaque at Manzanar was dedicated in April 1973 after a year-long debate over terminology.

of Manzanar, Mary Kageyama, who worked inside their home in Garden Grove to raise their five children. The couple was returning home from a trip to Sacramento in 1972 when they decided to visit a museum in the Inyo County city of Independence, just six miles north of Manzanar, because they'd heard it included information about the former camp. "We wanted to see what it was about," Mary recalled.

At that time, there wasn't much about Japanese American incarceration in the Eastern California Museum—maybe "one photo propped in a corner," she said—but the visit planted the seeds of a strong friendship between the Nomuras and Henry Raub, the museum's director. Shi volunteered to bring more items related to Manzanar, and Henry was happy to receive them.

Soon Shi became a one-man collections manager for the institution. He gathered photographs and possessions from his and Mary's families and friends. There were personal snapshots but also photos taken by professional photographers Ansel Adams and Toyo Miyatake. Over time, the Nomuras also developed a relationship with Pete Merritt, son of Ralph Merritt, the former project director for Manzanar. Now items were coming from those who had worked in camp administration as well.

Bill Michael, who served as the director of the museum from 1985 to 2005, recalled that "virtually no one" was doing this kind of historical collecting of Manzanar's past in the 1970s. He further described the collection as "groundbreaking." In addition to gathering material for the museum, Shi also constructed exhibition panels on his own.

At one point the Nomuras contemplated retiring to nearby Lone Pine and they even briefly opened a little gift store in the picturesque town ten miles south of Manzanar. Ultimately, however, they decided to stay in Southern California near their expansive extended family, but Manzanar always remained close to Shi's heart, and he made frequent trips to the museum to augment his collection there. According to Michael, Shi felt strongly that the Manzanar images and items needed to be close to where they had originated. In the end, Shi had amassed between seven hundred and eight hundred photographs, as well as a handful of artifacts.

THE DEBATE ABOUT TERMINOLOGY

On November 11, 1994, the Japanese American National Museum (JANM) opened an exhibition titled "America's Concentration Camps: Remembering the Japanese American Experience." The curator was Karen Ishizuka, whose husband, Robert Nakamura, and extended family had been incarcerated in Manzanar.

While many academics and government officials (including President Franklin D. Roosevelt) had for years referred to the ten detention centers as "concentration camps" in various contexts, this descriptor became a point of contention when the exhibition was to be mounted at New York's Ellis Island Museum, a National Park Service site. As the region was home to a significant Jewish population, authorities feared that the use of the term "concentration camp" would disrespect the wartime experience of Jews who were exterminated in death camps in Europe during World War II.

This debate was not a new one. In fact, during a hearing of the Commission on Wartime Relocation and Internment of Civilians (CWRIC) in Los Angeles on August 4, 1981, attorney Frank Chuman disputed the idea that the centers in which Japanese Americans had been detained were not "concentration camps." In response to statements by Senator S. I. Hayakawa, a respected semanticist and a Japanese Canadian, Chuman testified, "I'm going to have to take issue with him on that, because all of the camps were surrounded by barbed wires; there were watch towers; there were military jeeps, shotguns, rifles; and if anybody tried to get out of there without permission, they were ordered shot on sight."

A number of former Manzanar incarcerees were aligned with Chuman on this issue; even small businessman Shi Nomura, in his home-grown exhibition at the Eastern California Museum, consistently used the term "concentration camp" in his text panels. That said, the community was by no means united on the topic. Grace Pastries' owner George Izumi, who had worked in the mess hall in Manzanar, was among those flatly against the "concentration camp" label. He, in fact, publicly stated that he regretted donating personal items to JANM because of their preference for that terminology.

Densho, a nonprofit organization based in Seattle that was established to document the World War II story of Japanese Americans, has also adopted the use of "concentration camp" instead of the more widely used "internment camp." According to Densho's policy: "'Internment' refers to the legally permissible detention of enemy aliens in time of war. It is problematic when applied to American citizens; yet two-thirds of the Japanese Americans incarcerated were U.S. citizens."

Rangers at Manzanar National Historic Site also have moved away from the word "internment" to describe what the federal government did to U.S. citizens of Japanese ancestry. They are open to the variety of ways in which visitors talk about World War II history and its continuing relevance, but beyond trying to use words as they are defined, the rangers do not subscribe to a set terminology. "Being mindful of words is part of being a professional interpreter and historian," says Manzanar National Historic Site's chief of interpretation Alisa Lynch. "We preserve these sites and their stories in all of their controversy and complexity. Prescribing words doesn't help, but encouraging research and reflection does."

As for JANM's traveling exhibition, it opened on Ellis Island on April 3, 1998, its original title intact after many meetings, discussions, and negotiations. The only notable addition was a text panel placed at the beginning of the exhibition that described the definition of a concentration camp as "a place where people are imprisoned not because of any crimes they committed, but simply because of who they are."

ACTIVISM AT THE LOCAL LEVEL AND BEYOND

In 1972, military veteran and real estate agent Paul Bannai ran for Gardena City Council. He had done well in business and thought it was time to get involved in community service. His entire family— wife Hideko and children Kathryn, Don, and Lorraine—all helped in the campaign, whether it meant canvassing door to door, stuffing envelopes, or wrapping fortune cookies with the message "Bannai for You in '72."

The city already had a Japanese American councilman, Ken Nakaoka, who had been Bannai's high school classmate and his first employer in real estate. Nakaoka had been elected in 1966 and now was mayor. Following in Nakaoka's footsteps, Bannai easily won a seat in the city, which had a sizeable Japanese American population.

Even though a seat on the city council was a nonpartisan position, Bannai's Republican status was not lost on political observers. When the popular California assemblyman L. E. Townsend, who represented the historically Democratic 67th District, died in office in May 1973, Bannai was tapped to run as a token Republican in the special election that would occur the next month. His parents, who were still alive, gave their blessing and encouragement. "Without expecting to win, my name was entered," Bannai said in a 1989 interview for the California State Archives' State Government Oral History Program.

Also on his side were a few political heavyweights, namely the state governor at the time, Ronald Reagan. Bannai, in fact, had campaigned for Reagan in his bid for the governorship in 1966. He, like Reagan, had been a registered Democrat but later changed parties for "philosophical reasons."

To show his support, Reagan attended Bannai's fundraiser at a restaurant in El Segundo, and Bannai went on to beat his opponent, Torrance City treasurer Tom Ruppert, 54.9 percent to 42.5 percent. With this victory, Bannai became the first Japanese American in the California State Legislature, where he served until 1980.

Bannai was officially a Republican, but he did not run his office as an ideologue. He was conservative on law-and-order issues yet progressive on certain civil rights issues. He retained the staff of his late Democratic predecessor, and he socialized with the Democratic assembly speaker Bob Moretti. He was often approached by people on either side of the political spectrum who knew he could be a "point of interchange" between opposing forces.

While Bannai and other politicians were changing history by working within the system, many grassroots activists, in contrast, did not believe that electoral politics, compromise, or assimilating into the mainstream were the answer to achieving full equality in America. In New York City, Kazu Iijima and Shiz "Minn" Matsuda, two Nisei women who had been inspired by both the Black Power and antiwar movements, formed Asian Americans for Action (AAA or Triple A) in 1969, with the aim to promote pride and to mobilize political action among Asian Americans as a whole. Among those who became active with Triple A was the once aspiring dancer Aiko Herzig-Yoshinaga, who had moved with her daughter, Gerrie, to Los Angeles, learned

Aiko Herzig-Yoshinaga (*standing at far right*) with other members of Asian Americans for Action (Triple A) and staff from UCLA's Asian American Studies Center during a trip to New York City, c. 1973.

stenography there, and then made her way to the East Coast, where she remarried, had two more children, and then divorced.

Getting involved with Triple A in her early forties drastically awakened and evolved Aiko's political consciousness. "I was really struck by my ignorance about political systems and about racism," she said in an interview with Densho. Soon she started wondering about how these forces had affected her own life. "Being a member of Triple A at that particular time was the door that opened me for the future and how I would live," she said.

She began working as an office manager for an organization in Harlem whose focus was to instill a love of jazz among inner-city youth. Launched by pianist Billy Taylor, Jazzmobile recruited many of Taylor's world-renowned colleagues—among them Herbie Hancock, Max Roach, and Dizzy Gillespie—to spend Saturdays teaching jazz to children. Through her daily interactions with members of the black community, Aiko began to better understand and empathize with the sentiments of the black community, and in particular the importance of speaking out.

Soon Aiko was organizing workshops on Japanese American identity and history, and she participated in several antiwar demonstrations on the streets of New York City. Her first march with Triple A had been quite devastating, as she and fellow marchers were showered with slurs and other racist vitriol such as "Gooks!" and "Go back to where you came from!" "Just hateful things," she reported in an interview with JANM. "It was hard for me to take."

Newspaper photographers aimed their cameras on these agitating Asian Americans, who were breaking the model-minority archetype of being docile and quiet. The next day, the *Village Voice* featured a photo of the Triple A marchers, with Aiko right in the center.

"The family is going to find out about this one," she thought.

Meanwhile in Chicago, William Hohri was working in computer programming and, more importantly, was making waves in his community. His training ground the church—specifically the Northern Illinois Conference of the United Methodist Church, which was committed to reforming the organization and making it more open to issues of social justice. There was an administrative obstacle, however: anyone who wanted to advocate for a certain platform had to be willing to present it in person to the organization's thousand members. Hohri was not a natural public speaker; he'd get stage fright and his voice wavered when he appeared in front of large groups. And yet, undeterred, he kept speaking up. A momentous opportunity came in 1966, when black civil rights leader James Meredith was shot by a white gunman on the second day of his solo 220-mile March Against Fear from Memphis, Tennessee, to Jackson, Mississippi. Meredith survived but sustained multiple injuries and was unable to complete the march. When word of the incident spread, the Northern Illinois Conference was in session and put out a call for two of its members to join other volunteers who were going to continue the last leg of Meredith's march into Jackson. Since it fell on a Sunday, none of the clergy could attend. After some hesitation, Hohri raised his hand. "I guess I can go."

Hundreds of demonstrators participated in the March Against Fear in support of the civil rights activist James Meredith, Jackson, Mississippi, 1966.

Totally unfamiliar with the South, Hohri traveled by himself to Jackson and made his way to the march. When an airport cab driver asked where he was headed, Hohri pointed to his camera. "I'm going to take some pictures," he said, without revealing any more details. He was nervous about what would happen if he told the white driver he was going to be an active participant in the march.

At the protest, he was given a little plastic American flag to carry. "It was the first time in my life that I felt proud to be an American," said Hohri, explaining how his spirit was lifted as he witnessed thousands of white, black, and even Asian people walking in unity.

While living in Chicago with his wife and children, Hohri had not been active with any secular Japanese American groups. Chicago had a JACL chapter, but he had never been a supporter of the organization, which he viewed as being accommodationist, and yet he was inspired to get involved when he heard that the JACL national convention was to be held in Chicago in 1970. Reacting to that news, he and some other critics created a more progressive chapter, which they named the Chicago Liberation Chapter.

At the JACL convention, Hohri learned about several efforts that would later shape the future of the Japanese American community, as well as the larger social justice movement. Hohri heard about, for instance, a resolution introduced by San Francisco–based Nisei Edison Uno—a camp survivor himself—who had proposed reparations be paid to Japanese Americans who had been held by the government during World War II. Also included in the resolution was a $400 million fund that the government would allocate for community education projects. Although adopted by the JACL national council, the resolution failed to produce tangible results at the time; it did, however, plant the seed for later redress efforts.

More successful was the campaign to repeal Title II of the Internal Security Act of 1950. In the midst of the Black Power and antiwar movements, activists feared that the U.S. government might again attempt to round up and imprison individuals whom it viewed as threats to national security. The first public pilgrimage to Manzanar had been partially motivated by efforts to repeal Title II, and many other efforts to engage people in support of this issue spread throughout the nation.

The repeal bill was finally passed by Congress and signed by President Nixon on September 25, 1971. While the bill's passage was largely symbolic, as budget allocation for such camps had ceased back in 1957, it proved to Japanese Americans that despite their relatively low position on the political ladder, they could still unite for a common cause.

PROGRESS AND BACKLASH

In 1975, John Tateishi—who as a child had thought "America" meant the place outside of Manzanar—became a member of the JACL, an organization that his Kibei-Nisei father had disapproved of during World War II. Now, however, John had his father's full support, in part because the organization was focusing more on redress efforts in the wake of Edison Uno's failed 1970 resolution calling for the government to pay restitution to Japanese Americans. Other organizations seeking redress included E.O. 9066, Inc., named after the executive order that had made the mass incarcerations possible.

At the JACL's national convention in 1978, John Tateishi was appointed chairman of the National Redress Committee, and he wasted no time in getting the word out about the group's mandate. From the convention hotel, he faxed a press release to media outlets announcing that the JACL, on behalf of Japanese Americans, was demanding $25,000 per incarcerated person and the creation of an educational trust fund. "My whole strategy was we needed to fight this out in the public arena because most people in this country knew nothing about it, and most who did know felt that it was for our own good—it was protection against mobs and lynching. I wanted the public to understand that this issue was not about us, but it was about the Constitution," Tateishi said in an interview for the documentary *Three Lenses: Born Free and Equal*.

Another key group he needed to win over was the Nisei themselves. Not used to speaking about their suffering and pain, the Nisei also

JACL redress representative John Tateishi, c. 1980.

had to face accusations that they were simply being money hungry. "The [public] reactions were 'How dare they demand money; they're the ones who bombed Pearl Harbor,'" said Tateishi. "I knew that was going to happen, but it was [an] opportunity to start the dialogue."

Tateishi's intent was to vindicate the Nisei generation—"to break their silence, to begin to heal"—but they didn't see it that way. They released their fury in letters, phone calls, and personal visits to the JACL office in San Francisco. One day, Tateishi received a Nisei visitor who exclaimed, "You son of a bitch! Goddamn, you're going to make us talk."

The movement gained momentum as more Japanese Americans were elected to the U.S. Congress and more of them—along with many political allies not of Japanese descent[1]—joined the cause for redress. It started to look like actual federal legislation might be possible. Instead of demanding monetary reparations first, these members

---

1. Some of the early bills were, in fact, introduced by politicians with no Japanese ancestry.

of Congress advocated for the creation of a commission to hear testimony about the wartime experiences of Japanese Americans. Tateishi and the JACL supported this effort.

This strategy was not embraced by all members of the Japanese American community, however. One notable objector was Chicago-based William Hohri, who in 1979 joined forces with others in Seattle and San Francisco to create a new organization, the National Council for Japanese American Redress (NCJAR). Hohri, having abandoned his Chicago Liberation Chapter within the JACL long ago, worried that the movement would die under the weight of governmental commission hearings. Hohri made the rounds on talk radio all over the country and remembers it being a challenging responsibility: "It took its toll on me, so I'd limit myself to one [interview] a day. If I did two a day, I would just be worn out. It's the adrenaline, because [there's] a lot of hostility."

In response, Hohri realized how important it was for him to respond with strength. "You cannot be a nice Japanese American. You have to be very aggressive yourself," he said. "If you don't do that, you get chewed up."

Meanwhile, another grassroots organization had arisen in Los Angeles, home of the largest population of Japanese Americans. Alan Nishio, now an administrator at California State University, Long Beach, served as one of the leaders of the Little Tokyo People's Rights Organization (LTPRO), comprising largely Sansei activists committed to self-determination. LTPRO and members of the Manzanar Committee formed the core of a new Los Angeles–based group, the National Coalition for Redress/Reparations (NCRR), which was officially established in 1980.

Like NCJAR, the NCRR was initially against the commission hearings, although for slightly different reasons. Their objection was to the idea that the community's elders—some of whom had stayed completely silent about their experiences in the camps—would now be forced to not only speak out but to present evidence that they had been wronged, even though it was already obvious that they had been. Also, who would choose the speakers, and how? Would the former

A large delegation from the NCRR lobbies for redress and reparations in Washington, D.C., 1987.

incarcerees be represented only by those who were privileged, educated, and able to speak English?

With so many strong personalities, ideologies, and strategies at play, the community struggled to find common ground. Fortunately, their efforts were ultimately successful, and on July 31, 1980, President Jimmy Carter signed into law the Commission on Wartime Relocation and Internment of Civilians Act (CWRIC). The commission initially had one year and $1 million to produce a comprehensive report; time was of the essence.

A few months later, however, Democrat Carter lost his reelection bid to Republican Ronald Reagan, whose victory heralded a new wave of conservatism. Under this change, Japanese Americans worried progress to achieve redress and reparations might stall or be undone. Public sentiment toward Japan had also changed dramatically from the Cold War period to the 1980s; reactionary political pundits now bashed Japan as competitive imports challenged the dominance of

America's car industry. As before, Japanese Americans were often seen as agents of Japan, no matter how many generations they had been in the United States, and discrimination remained a problem.

Los Angeles's Gardena Buddhist Church had itself suffered from this negativity, including three incidents of arson in two years. In the first fire, in July 1980, the temple was completely destroyed. The congregation then raised funds and began to rebuild, only to be targeted by an arsonist a second time, in November 1981; that blaze almost completely undid all the restoration efforts. A third fire was set in February 1982, but fortunately it was discovered quickly and localized to the sanctuary. Elsewhere in the area, fires had damaged another Japanese Buddhist temple, two Catholic churches, a Baptist church, and a Presbyterian one. But Gardena, which suffered $1 million in losses, was the hardest hit.

The Nagatomi family, who had set out for the Gardena Buddhist Church from Manzanar in 1945, were no longer there. After being diagnosed with cancer in the late 1950s, Shinjo Nagatomi, the patriarch minister, and his wife, Sumi, had moved to San Francisco for treatment. He died in 1958, and Sumi passed away three years later from a massive stroke. Their son, Masatoshi, who had been sent to college in Japan shortly before World War II, was now a well-respected professor of Buddhist studies at Harvard. The three sisters—Dee, Shirley, and Jean—had all become teachers in Northern California.

After the third arson incident, the police installed a barbed wire fence and a twenty-four-hour TV monitor system to guard the site while it was rebuilt.[2] No one knew if the temple was being targeted because it represented Japan and/or Japanese Americans, but the threat remained, and in a nation in which mainstream society often ignored distinctions between nationalities, all people of Asian descent were vulnerable. In the summer of 1982, in fact, a young Chinese American man, Vincent Chin, was beaten to death with a baseball bat by two men, one of whom worked for a Detroit car manufacturer,

2. Lane Ryo Hirabayashi, "Community Lost? The Significance of a Contemporary Japanese American Community in Southern California," in *Asians in America: A Reader,* edited by Malcolm Collier (Dubuque, IA: Kendall-Hunt, 1992), 169–83.

in a horrific example of scapegoating over the trade war with Japan. This incident spurred a rallying cry among Asian American activists who viewed Chin's death as representative of the more widespread and systemic racism they experienced in the 1980s.

Even months after the third fire at the Buddhist temple, Dave Nakamura, a detective with the Gardena Police Department, told the *Los Angeles Times* that there were no suspects and no motive could be determined. "The investigation is very close to being at a very dead end," he said.[3]

And then that very month there was a break in the case. A forty-nine-year-old man, John Alden Stieber, came forward and confessed to Gardena police. Stieber, who had spent time in a mental institution, was declared insane. According to psychiatrists, he said he had set the fires to stop a conspiracy by the Catholic Church, the Bank of America, and the Japanese people to take over the nation.

UNCOVERING A COVER-UP

In 1978, Aiko Herzig-Yoshinaga moved from New York City to Washington, D.C., with her new husband, Jack Herzig. Jack, who had served with the U.S. Army's Counterintelligence Corps in Japan and other governmental agencies, was working with a nonprofit organization, and Aiko, now in her fifties and with her three children all fully grown, had time on her hands. One day, she decided to go to the National Archives to see if the FBI had a file on her antiwar activity in New York City. Nothing. Then she inquired about the government's files on her family while they were in camp.

Thus began Aiko's odyssey of gathering research about the incarceration of Japanese Americans, including those who had been imprisoned before President Roosevelt released his executive order in February 1942. Aiko, who had befriended writer Michi Weglyn back in New York, first used the footnotes in Michi's groundbreaking

---

3. Mary Curtis, "Arson-Plagued Church Revived," *Los Angeles Times,* July 8, 1982.

book, *Years of Infamy: The Untold Story of America's Concentration Camps* (1976), to dig into the archives. One file led to another and soon Aiko was following a paper trail to discover the truth behind the government's decision to incarcerate its own citizens. After Jack Herzig retired, he joined Aiko's efforts, and using his background in counterintelligence, he spoke out against the idea that intercepted Japanese diplomatic cables were proof of Japanese American disloyalty and therefore justified the camps, as many had claimed for years. Both Aiko and Jack joined William Hohri's NCJAR, which was now attempting to file a class-action suit against the U.S. government. The Herzigs' research and connections in D.C. would prove invaluable, and in recognition of that work the commission asked Aiko to join the CWRIC as a researcher.

The Herzigs' work did much to enhance the investigative work of legal historian Peter Irons, who was now teaching political science at the University of California, San Diego, while simultaneously investigating three separate U.S. Supreme Court decisions involving violations of governmental exclusion orders. Irons worked on behalf of

Aiko Herzig-Yoshinaga and Jack Herzig. c. 1997.

three Nisei men—Gordon Hirabayashi in Seattle, Fred Korematsu in San Francisco, and Minoru "Min" Yasui in Portland—and although each had different extenuating circumstances, Irons argued that they had all been illegally imprisoned. In three separate incidents, the men had been arrested for violating curfew, orders to report for detention, or both. Each had challenged his conviction in court during World War II, citing the unconstitutionality of the exclusion order, and each had failed to have his conviction overturned. The government cited "military necessity" as the justification for removing Japanese Americans from the West Coast.

While researching at the National Archives in Washington, D.C., Irons came across a memo from a Justice Department attorney, Edward Ennis, stating that the government had suppressed important confidential reports from the Supreme Court in the deliberation of the Korematsu case in 1944. Specifically problematic was General John L. DeWitt's "Final Report: Japanese Evacuation from the West Coast, 1942," which presented the reasons why the removal of this group of people was a "military necessity."

Assistant Secretary of War John McCloy, who supported the incarceration of Japanese Americans and had helped draft Executive Order 9066, received one of ten original copies of DeWitt's report on April 19, 1943. He became immediately alarmed after reviewing what it said. While the War Department had argued that mass removal was necessary because there was not enough time for separate hearings for individual Japanese Americans, DeWitt had written, "It was not that there was insufficient time in which to make determination; it was simply a matter of facing the realities that a positive determination could not be made, that an exact separation of the 'sheep from the goats' was unfeasible."

As this statement contradicted their previous statements and could be interpreted as racist, the War Department halted any further distribution of the report. While DeWitt protested any editing of his words, McCloy was able to negotiate the replacement of the "sheep from the goats" paragraph with a revised statement. The War Department attempted to destroy all ten copies of the original version and eventually released the revised version—as if the first one had never existed—in January 1944, during the time attorneys were developing their respective arguments in the legal cases involving the three Nisei men.

Two Department of Justice attorneys, John Burling and Edward Ennis, were writing their legal briefs on behalf of the government when they discovered additional problems with the report. DeWitt had cited arguments to incarcerate based on false information that had been refuted by three federal agencies. The attorneys found themselves in a quandary: How in good conscience could they allow the Supreme Court to cite or rely on the fabricated allegations in the published report?

They added a footnote in the brief disavowing DeWitt's reports on ship-to-shore signaling from the West Coast and radio communications from the West Coast to Japanese submarines. The War Department—specifically Assistant Secretary of War McCloy—and Solicitor General Charles Fahy, who was the one to argue the case before the High Court, opposed the inclusion of the footnote and halted the printing of the brief. After some back-and-forth, the footnote was replaced with different, watered-down wording in the legal documents presented to the Supreme Court. The High Court ruled in favor of the government in all three cases.

Now almost forty years later, Aiko Herzig-Yoshinaga found herself digging through government records attempting to uncover what had been hidden for decades. Various government communications had mentioned that not all of the original reports had been destroyed; there was a chance that a missing tenth report was still in existence. One day, she was at the National Archives when her eye was caught by a publication sitting on the corner of an archivist's desk. "It was luck of the Irish, luck of Japanese," she later said in an interview with Densho.

As soon as she opened it, she knew what it was. "Pow, this is it," she said. She had found the missing tenth copy, which apparently had been mixed up with other government papers while it was being edited by McCloy's office. With this crucial piece of evidence in hand, Herzig-Yoshinaga was able to help challenge rulings of the highest court in the nation.

TELLING THEIR STORIES

As part of the redress and reparations movement, activists, especially on the West Coast, were canvassing the community for individuals who would be willing to share their firsthand experiences of incarceration. Hearings were scheduled for Washington, D.C., as well as in areas with notable Japanese American populations, including Los Angeles, San Francisco, Seattle, Chicago, New York, and Boston.[4] Serving as short-term executive director of the working staff was former California assemblyman Paul Bannai, who had been coaxed out of retirement to take the position for at least the duration of the hearings.

Alan Nishio, a founding member of the NCRR and among those who had initially been opposed to such hearings, now wanted to make sure they were at least open to all, especially average working people, who he knew could speak with "great strength and conviction." "Those kinds of real stories have a great deal of impact," he later said in an interview. He also noted how the hearings helped lift the taboo of talking about the years spent in the camps: "[The commission hearings] made it okay for people in the community to tell their story . . . . All of a sudden, it became more of a dinner-table conversation."

While testimony was taken from high-profile Japanese American leaders (and even well-known personalities from outside the community, such as Studs Terkel), the most moving accounts came—as Nishio desired and had predicted—from ordinary people, many of whom were sharing their experiences and thoughts for the first time.

John Tateishi, who had been close to his own father, was significantly impacted by the testimonies of Nisei men, especially those who broke down as they were recounting their personal histories. "Before that, I had never, ever seen a Nisei man cry in public. I've seen them drunk and start sobbing and telling their [stories] . . . but I had never seen a Nisei man cry in public like that, one after another." Tateishi,

---

4. During this same time, hearings were also scheduled in three locations in Alaska to receive testimony about the haphazard displacement of Aleuts from their homes on two Alaskan islands during a Japanese offensive in the region.

Left to right: Roy Nakano, Alan Takeshi Nishio, and Mike Murase testify at the redress hearings in Los Angeles, 1981.

who was there to monitor every hearing, had to take regular breaks outside to regain his own composure.

Some speakers had English-language translators or stood with someone who read a statement on their behalf. One of these individuals was Hannah Tomiko Holmes, who had been deaf since the age of two and had entered Manzanar at thirteen. She had been at the California School for the Deaf in Berkeley before she suddenly found herself completely isolated inside the concentration camp, which had inadequate support for someone like her. Her family transferred to the Tule Lake concentration camp, where a Helen Keller School for "handicapped children" was to be launched, but the school was unsuccessful and closed after a few months.

Gerald Sato, an attorney who was matched with Holmes at a gathering sponsored by the Japanese American Bar Association, read her written statement while she sat by him. "I felt terribly isolated from other children at Manzanar," she had written. "I could not communicate with them. Somehow, I managed to do work at the camouflage net factory, and I tried to continue my education on my own by reading a lot."

Holmes found it close to impossible to find placement in a facility outside of camp. One deaf school in Arkansas that had barred black students stalled in their response to Holmes's admission application, and others charged cost-prohibitive fees for nonresidents. Holmes was finally able to continue her education at the Illinois School for the Deaf, and she graduated from there in 1948. She realized that among her deaf Japanese American peers she was exceedingly lucky to have received an education, which would allow her greater independence as an adult—something that influenced her interest in redress as well. "Now we, the handicapped Nisei, do not want to be financial burdens on our parents or our children," she wrote in her statement, emphasizing the importance of reparations in furthering the independence of herself and others like her.

Hannah Tomiko Holmes ended her testimony by quoting a letter sent to her in 1943 by Helen Keller, who had written in response to the short-lived school in Tule Lake having been named after her. "War, change, and sorrow cannot take from us anything really noble, gracious and helpful in our lives," Keller had written.

Another testimony came from Charles Nagao, who, at the urging of his wife Mary, had moved with their twin daughters from Manzanar to Seabrook Farms in 1944. He was sixty-five now, a resident of Vineland, New Jersey, and was working as assistant manager of a glass manufacturing company when he testified in the New York hearing held at the Roosevelt Hotel.

Nagao shared his memories of the cross-country train trip from Reno, Nevada, to Philadelphia, Pennsylvania, and then the uncomfortable forty-five-minute trailer ride to Seabrook, in which they got "sick with nausea and headache from exhaust gas seepage." And the troubles did not end once they had arrived at their destination.

"Resettlement was made not without its problems," he shared. Company workers who wanted to shop in the nearby town of Bridgeton were asked to take a private bus, as a way of avoiding trouble, but Charles refused and took the public bus. "The mere thought of having my free movement denied upon just having left the concentration camp was repugnant," he said. "I was determined to pursue a lifestyle on the outside as a free American."

In Bridgeton, certain merchants discriminated against the Japanese Americans, especially the Issei who didn't speak English. In one incident at a bowling alley, some young employees refused to set pins for Nagao and his Nisei friends because they were viewed as "the enemy." But when Nagao told the boys that the group would be generous tippers, the pin-setters backed down and went to work.

According to Nagao, there was also a glass ceiling at Seabrook: "Any promotions to the top positions were made available to the Caucasians." Also, when a promotional sales campaign was announced, Nisei were separated into a segregated work group, and of the all-white group of leaders, only one was willing to take charge of the all-Nisei group. "It took some doings on our part to convince the management that the Nisei were capable in representing the company out in the marketing area," Nagao remembered.

Mary Nagao left her job at Seabrook Farms in 1956 to join the Cumberland County Clerk's Office. After working there for two decades, she hoped to be promoted to a supervisory position but was beat out by a white woman who had just joined the office. And in spite of both Charles and Mary's longtime service at Seabrook, neither was eligible for a pension because they had worked non-union positions.

Charles admitted that appearances were deceiving, and that even though many former incarcerees were now living what seemed to be good lives, they shared a dark history:

While during these thirty-nine years [since leaving camp] those of us who are at present pursuing a seemingly normal lifestyle 3,000 miles away from home on the West Coast, we were uprooted by our government by Executive Order 9066 and have endured humiliations and hardships by this wrongful act in incarcerating 110,000 people of Japanese ancestry into concentration camps without due trial.

Therefore, I trust the members of this distinguished commission will apprise the Congress of the United States of the government's wrongdoing and the necessity for its redress with recommendation of monetary compensation commensurate with this unprecedented act.

When the only Japanese American on the federally appointed commission,[5] Judge William Marutani, queried Charles Nagao on government reparations, he answered that funds should go to individuals as
well as to a community trust. But Nagao included this qualification:
"This does not mean that it is going to be [the] . . . amount of money
that would compensate for [the] amount of suffering that has been
caused by the uprooting of us from our homes."

Ernest Kinzo Wakayama, the World War I veteran and former
Terminal Islander, traveled all the way from Fukuoka, Japan, at age
eighty-six to testify before the CWRIC. This had been his first trip back
to the United States since leaving on a repatriation ship in 1946. "My
remaining life is now very short," he said. "I will say this: I was a real
American, and I still believe so. Who knows? Only God and my sons."

Probably the most dramatic incident occurred during the Los
Angeles testimony of Jim Kawaminami, president of the 442nd/100th
Veterans Association of Southern California. On August 5, 1981, he
first described the unsanitary and desolate conditions of the concentration camps and assembly centers. (He said the "stench" was "unbear-
able.") It was from within these places that the Nisei had volunteered
to serve in the U.S. military, explained Kawaminami, who presented
his organization's resolution recommending "equitable relief" for
victims.

He then began reading another document specifically challenging
the allegations of Lillian Baker, an outspoken opponent of redress and
reparations for Japanese Americans. A resident of Gardena, she was
the head of a group called Americans for Historical Accuracy.

Baker, who was in the audience and had testified previously in
Washington, D.C., got to her feet and attempted to tear the document
from Kawaminami's hands. At least three officers interceded and
Baker was evicted from the hearing to cheers from many in the crowd.

"Let's have some order," demanded Republican congressman Dan
Lungren, vice chair of the commission.

Kawaminami then replied, "Mr. Chairman, now you can all see
what kind of people we have to put up with."

---

5. Paul Bannai was part of the working staff.

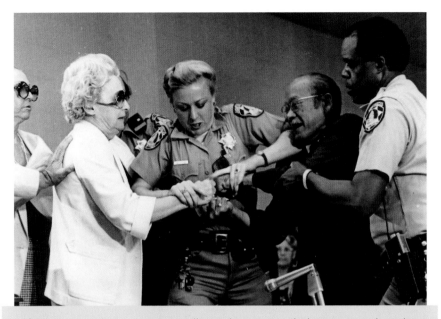

Officers assist Jim Kawaminami as Lillian Baker tries to take his papers at the redress hearings, Los Angeles, 1981.

When attorney Frank Chuman addressed the commission in Los Angeles in 1981, he brought up a rarely used "common law remedy" known as a writ of *coram nobis*, which he had learned as a law student in Maryland. Realizing how obscure it was, he even spelled out the Latin term for those in attendance. First used in the English legal system, *coram nobis* addresses situations when a serious error was unearthed that would have affected a court's original judgment.

Peter Irons, the lawyer who had been working on behalf of Japanese Americans incarcerated during wartime, knew the remedy well. Convicted and imprisoned for refusing to register for the draft during the Vietnam War, he had used *coram nobis* to successfully expunge his own conviction after records showed that the government had targeted him for the draft early because of his resistance. Now he was looking to use *coram nobis* to reverse decisions made by the Supreme Court. Even with the lucky research assistance of Aiko Herzig-Yoshinaga, however, he needed even more help.

LEGAL REMEDIES

By the time of the CWRIC commission hearings, Paul and Hideko Bannai's daughters, Kathryn and Lorraine, were now attorneys. Kathryn, the oldest of the three Bannai children, worked in Seattle, while Lorraine, the youngest and newly graduated from the University of San Francisco, was at Minami, Tomine, and Lew, a small community law firm located on Lake Merritt in Oakland and led entirely by Asian American men not much older than her. In fact, one of the partners, Dale Minami, was also from Gardena and had been a family friend for years. For Lorraine, working there felt like going home.

As a young woman, and as one of the few minority female lawyers at the time, Lorraine was sometimes mistaken for either a court interpreter or even a plaintiff or defendant when she walked into court. She imagined opposing lawyers thinking, "Oh, this is going to be an easy win because I've got this quiet Asian woman on the other side." Time and again they were proven wrong.

The firm had an informal and fun yet committed corporate culture that fed off the community vibe; the street noise that filtered in was often the sounds of passing skateboards and the blare of boom boxes. Dedicated to community lawyering, they took on illegal police sweeps and university cutbacks in ethnic studies, along with representing high-profile clients such as Wendy Yoshimura, a Manzanar-born Sansei who was arrested with heiress Patty Hearst for crimes they allegedly committed as members of the Symbionese Liberation Army.

In the early years, money was always an issue, and the group sat around a table every month to decide which bills could no longer go unpaid. "It was very difficult obviously financially at times. But [there] was a wonderful sense of freedom and camaraderie around the firm," remembered Lorraine in an interview for Densho in March 2000. To relieve stress from their heavy caseload, Lorraine and Dale would go to the local ice cream parlor every day to play a round of the video game Space Invaders.

The team was also part of the Bay Area Attorneys for Redress (BAAR), a group of mostly Japanese American lawyers investigating constitutional violations during World War II. Lorraine testified at the CWRIC hearings, identifying three areas in which the executive, legislative, and judicial branches of government "wrongfully allowed the military to exercise control over civilians." She specifically questioned whether President Franklin D. Roosevelt had taken into consideration an intelligence communication referred to as the Munson Report before he signed Executive Order 9066. The Munson Report had maintained that Japanese Americans proved to be no security risk.

As was previously agreed upon, Paul Bannai left the commission after the hearings were conducted, making way for a new executive director, attorney Angus Macbeth, to spearhead the arduous task of synthesizing into a comprehensive summary the testimonies of 750 witnesses together with archival research. This task took more than a year.

In December 1982 the CWRIC released its 467-page report, *Personal Justice Denied*. The report, written in clear and understandable language, featured this statement: "The promulgation of Executive Order 9066 was not justified by military necessity, and the decisions which followed from it—detention, ending detention and ending exclusion—were not driven by analysis of military conditions. The broad historical causes which shaped these decisions were race prejudice, war hysteria and a failure of political leadership."

Around this time, Dale Minami received a phone call from legal historian Peter Irons. Irons had been doing research on the three Nisei Supreme Court cases in Washington, D.C., when he came across a memo from a Justice Department attorney stating that the government had suppressed important confidential reports.

Irons wanted to implement *coram nobis* to challenge the Supreme Court rulings of the Japanese American men he was working with, but he wasn't a litigator and needed members of BAAR to help. Dale went down the hallway to get Lorraine to join in the conversation with Irons. "I might not have known it exactly at that point in time," Lorraine told Densho, "but [I] certainly probably soon knew that this was just a tremendous opportunity, a case of a lifetime." She realized the importance of the case she was about to undertake in part because,

Press conference on the Korematsu case, 1983. *Seated, left to right:* Dale Minami, Fred Korematsu, and Peter Irons. *Standing:* Donald Tamaki, Dennis Hayashi, and Lorraine Bannai.

like other attorneys, she had studied the Fred Korematsu case in law school. "It involved my parents' internment, our parents' internment, Dale's family . . . . It was a case that would reopen not only Fred's individual case, but also the whole question about the internment in general."

Before long they were contacting the whole network of civil rights attorneys along the West Coast. While Dale would take the lead on the Korematsu case, Lorraine would help organize and review the evidence. Her sister, Kathryn, meanwhile, would be in charge of the Gordon Hirabayashi case in Seattle.

Several months later, on January 19, 1983, Korematsu filed a writ of *coram nobis*, which was followed two weeks later by filings by Hirabayashi and Yasui in their respective U.S. district courts. Department of Justice lawyer Victor Stone requested that the judge delay legal proceedings until the CWRIC released its recommendations. The announcement of those recommendations came in June 1983; they were an apology signed by the sitting U.S. president, the establishment of an educational fund for former incarcerees and their descendants, and the appropriation of $1.5 billion to be distributed as monetary reparations.

The *coram nobis* cases finally moved forward, with Minami arguing that Korematsu's conviction should be vacated because the government had suppressed vital information. Judge Marilyn Hall Patel immediately ruled from the bench to do just that, stating in her written ruling, "It stands as a caution that in times of distress the shield of military necessity and national security must not be used to protect governmental actions from close scrutiny and accountability." This decision was followed by the vacating of wartime convictions in both the Yasui and Hirabayashi *coram nobis* cases as well.

Despite these successes, the Supreme Court had still not ruled on the constitutionality of the wartime exclusion order. Hohri's NCJAR aimed for such a resolution and recruited twenty-five plaintiffs to challenge the government in a class-action lawsuit. The high court eventually heard *United States v. Hohri et al.* in 1987 and unanimously ruled to remand the case to a lower court. NCJAR did not find success in either the appeals court or in re-petitioning the Supreme Court,

NCJAR members on the day the Supreme Court held a hearing of the class-action lawsuit *United States v. Hohri et al.*, April 1987. *Left to right:* Fred Korematsu, Gordon Hirabayashi, Michi Weglyn, William Hohri, Aiko Herzig-Yoshinaga, and Harry Ueno. The red commemorative frame was handmade by Hannah Tomiko Holmes.

and Hohri's efforts to establish a legal precedent was ultimately foiled, leaving the door open for concentration camps to someday again be established in the United States.

In later reflecting on this series of legal efforts, Lorraine Bannai said, "I hope people see their own roles in being vigilant to protect communities under siege. During the war, Japanese Americans stood virtually alone[;] very few stood against their incarceration, and most silently let it happen. The failure to speak can lead to injustice."

A PATH TO SUCCESS

For the advocates of redress, the commission hearings, report, and recommendations were all undeniably crucial elements in advancing their campaign, but in some ways those were just previews of the battles that awaited them. When Republican Ronald Reagan was elected, many of the cause's supporters became despondent, believing that redress and reparations would probably be out of reach under the new president's conservative administration.

In response to these mumblings of defeat, John Tateishi of the JACL urged people to reconsider the situation. "Wait a minute," he said. "Reagan grew up in Southern California and had Japanese

The George Kiriyama family celebrate after George's mother, Sugi Kiriyama, received her redress check in Washington D.C.; Los Angeles, 1990. *Back, left to right:* George Kiriyama, Harry Honda, Haru Ikkanda (George's sister), Janice Trost (Haru's daughter), Sue Kunitomi Embrey, Iku Kato Kiriyama. *Front:* Sugi Kiriyama, traci kato-kiriyama.

American friends as he was growing up." His thought was that Reagan had at least some exposure to the Japanese American community, and in fact while serving as governor of California he had regularly interacted with not only Assemblyman Bannai but also another Japanese American legislator, Democrat Floyd Mori. By contrast, Jimmy Carter's Democratic administration included political aides from the South who might never have come in contact with an Asian American. "Reagan's people are from California," Tateishi mused. "This is a blessing in disguise."

In spite of this optimism, however, it would take five years of political wrangling, the introduction and failure of multiple congressional redress bills, and much community lobbying and organizing before Congress eventually passed the Civil Liberties Act of 1988. The bill apologized "on behalf of the nation" for the World War II mistreatment of Japanese Americans and authorized an educational fund and redress payments of $20,000 each to former incarcerees. President Reagan signed the bill into law at the White House on August 10, 1988.

Among the guests invited to witness this historic event was Charles Nagao, who had resettled in New Jersey with his family to work at Seabrook. His wife, Mary, had died three years earlier. "To test American citizens' rights without any evidence . . . is a terrible thing," Charles reflected. "These are the things we are fighting for in the redress—that they would not happen to any Americans, any time in the future."

William Hohri purchased a Nissan automobile with funds from his redress check, Chicago, 1991. He used this photo on his Christmas card that year, noting that "the [license] plates are the car's best accessory."

WESTERN DEFENSE COMMAND AND FOURTH ARMY
WARTIME CIVIL CONTROL ADMINISTRATION
Presidio of San Francisco, California
April 30, 1942

INSTRUCTIONS
TO ALL PERSONS OF
JAPANESE
ANCESTRY

Living in the Following Area:

All that portion of the County of Los Angeles, State of California, within the boundary beginning at the intersection of Western Avenue and Redondo Beach Boulevard; thence easterly on Redondo Beach Boulevard and Compton Boulevard to Atlantic Boulevard; thence northerly on Atlantic Boulevard to Artesia Street; thence easterly on Artesia Street to Alameda Street; thence southerly on Alameda Street to Carson Street; thence westerly on Carson Street to a point at which a northward line established by Western Avenue intersects Carson Street; thence northerly on said line and Western Avenue to the point of beginning.

Pursuant to the provisions of Civilian Exclusion Order No. 20, this Headquarters, dated April 30, 1942, all persons of Japanese ancestry, both alien and non-alien, will be evacuated from the above area by 12 o'clock noon, P. W. T., Thursday, May 7, 1942.

No Japanese person living in the above area will be permitted to change residence after 12 o'clock noon, P. W. T., Thursday, April 30, 1942, without obtaining special permission from the representative of the Commanding General, Southern California Sector, at the Civil Control Station located at:

1652½ South Western Avenue,
Torrance, California.

Such permits will only be granted for the purpose of uniting members of a family, or in cases of grave emergency.

The Civil Control Station is equipped to assist the Japanese population affected by this evacuation in the following ways:

1. Give advice and instructions on the evacuation.
2. Provide services with respect to the management, leasing, sale, storage or other disposition of most kinds of property, such as real estate, business and professional equipment, household goods, boats, automobiles and livestock.
3. Provide temporary residence elsewhere for all Japanese in family groups.
4. Transport persons and a limited amount of clothing and equipment to their new residence.

The Following Instructions Must Be Observed:

1. A responsible member of each family, preferably the head of the family, or the person in whose name most of the property is held, and each individual living alone, will report to the Civil Control Station to receive further instructions. This must be done between 8:00 A. M. and 5:00 P. M. on Friday, May 1, 1942, or between 8:00 A. M. and 5:00 P. M. on Saturday, May 2, 1942.

2. Evacuees must carry with them on departure for the Assembly Center, the following property:
   (a) Bedding and linens (no mattress) for each member of the family;
   (b) Toilet articles for each member of the family;
   (c) Extra clothing for each member of the family;
   (d) Sufficient knives, forks, spoons, plates, bowls and cups for each member of the family;
   (e) Essential personal effects for each member of the family.

All items carried will be securely packaged, tied and plainly marked with the name of the owner and numbered in accordance with instructions obtained at the Civil Control Station.

The size and number of packages is limited to that which can be carried by the individual or family group.

3. No pets of any kind will be permitted.

4. No personal items and no household goods will be shipped to the Assembly Center.

The United States Government through its agencies will provide for the storage, at the risk of the owner, of the more substantial household items, such as iceboxes, washing machines, pianos and other heavy furniture. Cooking utensils and other small items will be accepted for storage if crated, packed, sealed and plainly marked with the name and address of the owner. Only one name and address will be used by a given family.

CHAPTER FOUR

NEVERAGAIN

On a summer day in 1995, Jeanne Wakatsuki Houston and her adult daughter Cori sped up U.S. Highway 395 toward Manzanar, then a recent addition to the National Park Service's roster of national historic sites. This was Jeanne's second pilgrimage to Manzanar; the first was in 1971, when she and her husband James were collaborating on the memoir that became the award-winning *Farewell to Manzanar.*

Now, fifty years after her incarceration, Jeanne was returning to the Owens Valley to investigate a "remarkable pattern of 'displacement' [that had] occurred on this particular stretch of land in the high California desert." She had already confronted and healed—or so she thought—the trauma of her own family's wrenching displacement from Terminal Island and subsequent incarceration, but she also recognized the other people who had once been connected to this place. As a child at Manzanar, she had imagined ghosts of Indians riding bareback across the firebreak that served as her playground, and she ate fruit from trees that had been planted decades earlier by hopeful

traci kato-kiriyama at the 48th Annual Manzanar Pilgrimage, commemorating the seventy-fifth anniversary of the signing of E.O. 9066, April 2017.

Out Skirt—Manzanar, by Akio Ujihara, 1942.

farmers lured to the planned irrigation community called Manzanar
(Spanish for "apple orchard") by the promise of abundant water.

As the "purple and burnt mahogany cones" of the Alabama Hills
appeared outside her car window on this second visit, Jeanne was
taken aback by a flood of emotion. Although she tried to maintain a
light tone for her daughter's benefit, Jeanne's throat constricted and
her eyes welled with tears. "Hadn't years of therapeutic work and the
catharsis of writing *Farewell to Manzanar* with my husband healed
the trauma associated with World War II and the internment?" she
wondered. But then again, "Post-traumatic stress syndrome never goes
away, they say."

For Cori—and many other children of survivors—Manzanar had
persisted as a traumatic event in her mother's history but had little, if
any, direct personal meaning in her own life. And yet on this hot summer day, as Cori panned her video camera across the sagebrush scrub
landscape and tilted the lens toward the stalwart presence of Mount

Williamson, she would soon encounter tangible connections to Manzanar, and to family members she had never known in person.

Approaching the area near Block 28, where the Wakatsukis had once lived, Jeanne and Cori came upon a line of "gnarled, aged pear trees . . . still sprouting"—to their surprise!—"some sparse green leaves." Jeanne told Cori how her Issei grandfather had revived the trees by irrigating and pruning them, coaxing delicious pear crops for the family throughout their incarceration. When Cori brushed her fingertips over the weathered branches, she touched what her grandfather had touched, stood where he had stood, and felt his enduring presence.

On their drive home, with Manzanar receding from view, Cori left with a deeper connection to her family's history, while Jeanne enjoyed a "sense of liberation" from its burden, and even relief from its "dark energy." She had gained a new level of trust in her artistic intuition and felt ready to, in her words, "break through [the] barbed-wire confinement [she] had placed around [her] imagination."

It would take multiple repeat visits for John Tateishi to feel released from Manzanar's firm grip. He first returned in 1975, alone, and on a quest to find out why images of "fences and towers" kept appearing in the poetry he was then writing. "I realized that this thing . . . was really in my psyche, and I told my wife that I needed to go to Manzanar."

Tateishi hiked out to George Creek, where he used to spend hours listening to his grandfather chant in the hut he had crafted from tree branches. Standing there decades later, Tateishi realized, "I have never been free of this place . . . . I left Manzanar more than fifty years ago, but out there, somewhere on the deserts of America, I'm still a young boy running in the wind."

On another return visit, in 2010, "something snapped." He had been unable to make peace with Manzanar before, but this time was different: "I returned with . . . a group of young college-aged students [but] . . . I spent most of my time at the site by myself . . . . In a sense it kind of freed me from that place, so I've been back there several times since then and, you know, it's a trip . . . . It's not any kind of meaningful journey for me to go to Manzanar anymore . . . . Just that one time, it did change it for me."

"JOURNEY TO OUR COMMUNITY HEALING"

The hallmarks of visits like Wakatsuki Houston's and Tateishi's—confronting ghosts of a painful past, reclaiming family history, and finding a measure of release from lingering trauma—have likewise been shared by thousands of other survivors and their descendants who have found their way back to Manzanar. One mental health professional, Dr. Satsuki Ina, who was born in 1944 at Tule Lake, has explored the long-term psychological effects of incarceration in the camps. Speaking at the 46th Annual Manzanar Pilgrimage in 2015, Dr. Ina defined both the nature of the trauma and a partial path toward healing it. "This journey to Manzanar is the journey to our community healing," she said.

Beyond the outward and abundantly staggering losses of land, property, communities, and businesses, survivors suffered even more profound inward losses, which the resettlement years—including formal reparations—could not cure. According to Dr. Ina, this persistent trauma stems from the loss of "dignity [and] self-determination; of power, hope, faith; of possibility; [and] of pride in being Japanese." This loss remains "in the hearts and souls of survivors" and spans the generations. In the words of survivor Hank Umemoto, the mass incarceration "left a scar in my mind because we were told that we were Japs: whether we were born here or in the Land of the Rising Sun, we were Japs."

For Dr. Ina and others, an essential first step toward healing is to reject language that masks or minimizes the depth of the injustice and to replace it with more accurate terminology: "incarceration" instead of "internment"; "concentration camp" instead of "War Relocation Center"; and "forced relocation" instead of "evacuation." Other steps may include group therapy and raising public awareness through education, art, and community organizing.

FORMAL RECOGNITION

Manzanar seemed all but forgotten when Jeanne Wakatsuki Houston visited in 1995. Then one of the newest additions to the roster of the National Park Service (NPS), Manzanar National Historic Site was described by one *Washington Post* columnist as perhaps "the most neglected unit in the NPS."

Although Manzanar appeared overlooked and unkempt, the fact that it was even part of the National Park system represented years of heavy lifting. Sue Kunitomi Embrey and others had been steadfastly working toward this objective, beginning with a grassroots campaign for state historical recognition in 1971 and '72. Embrey later said in her published oral history, *Unquiet Nisei* (2007), that, in retrospect, the effort to have Manzanar recognized as a historic landmark at the state level was accomplished in a "very short time."

When the state historical plaque was dedicated during the Manzanar pilgrimage of 1973, nearly fifteen hundred people witnessed

Master stonemason and gardener Ryozo Kado at the internal police post he built at Manzanar, c. 1943.

Ryozo Kado installing the California State Historical Landmark plaque, 1973.

Ryozo Kado affix it to the stone sentry post he had originally constructed thirty years earlier. "They came on motorcycles, in [Mercedes Benzes] and junky little cars," Embrey recalled. "It was amazing!" With state landmark status secured—and redress gaining momentum—more Nisei started to attend the annual Manzanar pilgrimage. It was no longer just for so-called radicals like Sue Kunitomi Embrey or Karl and Elaine Black Yoneda.

Progress was being made, but the struggle was far from over. The next two objectives were achieving national historic landmark status and then full-fledged national historic site status. Only then, Sue and others realized, could the U.S. government no longer hide behind the justification of "military necessity," nor minimize its abrogation of the civil liberties of American citizens. Recognition and preservation of the site also meant that survivors and their descendants would have a place to touch the past and connect with their own ghost stories of Manzanar.

In 1991—eighteen years after the state historical plaque was dedicated, and three years after the successful passage of the Civil Liberties Act of 1988—Congress was poised to recognize Manzanar as a national historic site. The National Park Service could now formally recognize the wrongs of the U.S. government and, in acknowledging those mistakes, show how the country might come to terms with its past. As Embrey asserted, Manzanar "can and must be a positive model of what our nation is willing to do and to shout to the world that our people are strong and resolute, and that we will acknowledge the errors of the past."

But while the nation was ready to make Manzanar a national historic site, the Owens Valley largely was not. Some residents simply could not get beyond the rationalization that "military necessity" had required that a "Jap camp" be put in their midst in the first place. Further, local Owens Valley Paiute required that any interpretative displays at the park also include stories of their own connection to the site, including their forced relocation from the valley in the mid-1800s. Also complicating matters, the Japanese American community was by no means united on how Manzanar's story should be told.

Once again, terminology was front and center in the debate: Would the National Park Service refer to Manzanar as a concentration camp? Or would it stick with the site's proper historical name of Manzanar War Relocation Center? Sue Embrey, relieved that her goal was in sight, would be content to simply call it by its new name: Manzanar National Historic Site.

Of all the factors that needed to be considered and negotiated, however, the one that slowed authorization to a thirteen-month crawl through Congress was the decades-old struggle over water rights in the Owens Valley. The Los Angeles Department of Water and Power (DWP) still owned most of the land on which Manzanar stood, and they jealously guarded the associated water rights, balking at the idea of transferring any land until the NPS was specifically excluded from having authority over how the DWP used the valley's water or mitigated associated environmental impacts.

As it turned out, the final hurdle of turning the site into a national park was the dust that had been, according to one former inmate, "the central fact of life" at Manzanar. The infamous dust storms of the 1940s were a result of DWP's having drained Owens Lake dry in the mid-1920s, and now that the Owens Valley's poor air quality had become a pressing environmental concern, the DWP feared that the NPS would require stricter dust mitigation standards than it was then prepared to enforce.

With Rose Ochi acting as liaison on behalf of Los Angeles mayor Tom Bradley, and despite DWP foot-dragging, the end was in sight by Remembrance Day of 1992. On February 18 of that year, the House of Representatives passed HR 543, and a companion bill passed the

Senate the following day. On March 3, 1992, President George H. W. Bush signed the bill into law, creating Manzanar National Historic Site. The DWP continued to stall transfer of the land to the NPS for five more years, until a three-way land swap was worked out between the NPS, the Bureau of Land Management (BLM), and the DWP.

Finally, in 2000 the Clinton administration provided over $4 million in funding to preserve sites related to the forced removal of Japanese Americans, the majority of which was earmarked for Manzanar. This was the foundation for something tangible to be built and produced on this place of pilgrimage, memory, and conscience. Manzanar would forever after be "a visible reminder of the internment," said Senator Daniel Akaka on the day it became a national historic site. Its essential purpose was this: "to avoid a repetition of the past."

SACRIFICE AND LOYALTY

In September 2001, while Sue Embrey and other members of the Manzanar National Historic Site Advisory Commission, authorized by Congress, were guiding the shape of new exhibits at Manzanar, twelve-year-old Sean Miura had just moved with his family to New Jersey, not far from Manhattan. His mother, Kathryn, had been part of the Hirabayashi *coram nobis* legal team, while his Aunt Lorraine had represented Korematsu.

"I was in third period English class and heard a low-flying plane," Miura recalled. "This was September 11, 2001."

Two fuel-laden jetliners piloted by terrorists struck the twin towers in lower Manhattan, killing nearly three thousand men, women, and children, and striking a blow at the heart of the nation's financial center. As part of the synchronized attack orchestrated by Al-Qaeda leader Osama bin Laden, a third jetliner crashed into the Pentagon building outside Washington, D.C., just a short time later. While a fourth plane was still airborne over Pennsylvania—its target presumed to be either the White House or the U.S. Capitol—U.S. Army Colonel J. Edgar Wakayama was busy at work inside a secure, windowless section of the Pentagon. He had been recalled to active duty to investigate the attack on the USS *Cole* the previous year.

A colleague shouted, "Ed, you got to evacuate; something's happening at the Twin Towers in New York and [here at] the Pentagon." As Col. Wakayama stepped outside into an emergency assembly area in the center of the Pentagon, he smelled jet fuel and saw black, billowing smoke. Although he was ordered to evacuate, Wakayama insisted his medical background might be of some use if he stayed to help. He had served as a medic in the Vietnam War, and jumping into the fray was second nature to him.

Col. Wakayama entered the Pentagon twice to search for injured people and lead them to safety. On his third attempt, the heat was overwhelming and he knew there would be no more survivors. He then turned his attention to the hastily erected first aid stations and began administering intravenous fluids to injured victims. "Look, this is what you see in combat," he told other rescue workers. "Get used to it." He worked on-site for the next ten days, stopping only to call his family each night.

Emergency response at the Pentagon, September 11, 2001.

Army Reserve Colonel J. Edgar Wakayama (*right*) receives his citation for the Soldier's Medal from Tom Christie, director of operational test and evaluation for the Office of the Secretary of Defense, May 2002. The medal is the army's highest honor for non-combat heroism.

In December 2001 Wakayama was awarded the Soldier's Medal, the highest award for non-combat valor. "I wasn't a hero," he told his staff. "I was just doing what I was trained to do."

The unlikely path that placed U.S. Army Colonel J. Edgar Wakayama in the Pentagon when American Airlines Flight 77 struck the west side of the building had begun fifty-eight years earlier at Manzanar, when Junro Edgar Wakayama became one of 541 babies born in camp. His middle name came from the attorney Edgar Camps, who had filed a writ of *habeas corpus* on behalf of his mother, Toki, while she and his father, Ernest, were imprisoned at Santa Anita Assembly Center.

When Edgar was two, his parents renounced their U.S. citizenship and the family moved to Japan, but Edgar eventually returned to the states as a draftee during the Vietnam War, even though he didn't fully believe in the cause. He later said he joined the military not only to please his father, a World War I veteran, but also to be able to honor the sacrifices made by Japanese Americans soldiers of World War II. "They volunteered from a concentration camp," he said. "They decided to risk their lives to serve their country, and I cannot really betray them."

Edgar served a tour of duty in Vietnam and then remained a reserve officer in the Army Medical Service Corps. He later went on to serve in Operations Desert Shield and Desert Storm from August 2, 1990, to February 28, 1991. At the time of 9/11, Wakayama was investigating the safety of military equipment, including armor-plated artillery shells that contain depleted uranium, and he often found himself at loggerheads with military defense contractors who resented his scrupulous attention to detail and utter disregard for their opinions. "It didn't bother me to get criticized," he stated. "I was just telling the truth."

In the months that followed the attacks on the World Trade Center and the Pentagon, youngster Sean Miura witnessed firsthand what he called "a culture of racism and xenophobia not unlike that which existed in 1941." Coworkers told Col. Wakayama, "This is how the people felt on December 7, 1941, against the Japanese."

On the streets, in schools, and outside their mosques, Arab Americans and Muslims experienced a new level of scrutiny, suspicion, and overt racism. In the interest of national security, the U.S. government enacted sweeping domestic policies that threatened civil liberties in ways that were eerily familiar to many Japanese Americans.

Immediately after 9/11, U.S. federal agents detained two thousand people of Arab, Muslim, and South Asian heritage, and on October 23 of that year President George W. Bush signed into law the Patriot Act (an acronym for the formal name Provide Appropriate Tools Required to Intercept and Obstruct Terrorism), which gave the government the authority to conduct mass surveillance without specific evidence of wrongdoing.

The next fall, on the one-year anniversary of 9/11, the U.S. government enacted a screening and tracking program (the National Security Entry-Exit Registration System, or NSEERS) that applied to non-citizen non-residents from predominantly Muslim countries. Although the domestic-registration portion lasted only a little over a year and the entry-and-exit program was suspended in 2011 when the Department of Homeland Security delisted the specific countries in question, the basic structure for a national "Muslim registry" has remained in place and has been the source of much discussion during the first year of President Donald Trump's administration.

Col. Wakayama spoke out against the Patriot Act and freely shared his story with school groups and at other public gatherings. It was an already familiar role for the activist, who had been speaking to audiences about his experiences in Manzanar for decades. When he first moved to Massachusetts in 1962 to attend Northeastern University, Wakayama was invited to speak at the local Grange, and when he

Edgar Wakayama outside his Las Vegas home, 2004. He returned to Manzanar as a guest lecturer in June 2009, sixty-six years after he was born there.

Above left: Ernest Kinzo Wakayama, age 96, received the Department of Veterans Affairs' 75th World War I anniversary medal. He is pictured here in front of the U.S. flag given to him on his ninety-first birthday by Congressman Norman Mineta, who was incarcerated at the Heart Mountain camp during World War II. The flag flew over the U.S. Capitol building on June 17, 1988, Ernest's birthday.

Above right: National Memorial Cemetery of the Pacific, at Punchbowl Crater in Hawai'i, 2017.

told the audience that he had been born in Manzanar, California, near Death Valley, most had never heard of it and insisted there was "no such thing" as an American concentration camp. Wakayama opened their eyes to the truth of his birthplace and was soon invited back to address an even larger group.

He returned to his birthplace in 2009 and shared his story once more, seeking to pass on two key messages to the next generation: "Always question authority" and, evoking Winston Churchill, "Never give up."

In keeping with this adage, he also made sure that his father, Ernest Wakayama, received a 75th World War I anniversary medal from the Department of Veteran's Affairs before he died. Following his father's passing, at age 102, he arranged for Ernest's burial with full military honors at the National Memorial Cemetery of the Pacific (Punchbowl) in Hawai'i.

SPEAKING OUT

John Tateishi led the JACL as national director in the early and mid-1980s and then stepped back shortly before the passage of the Civil Liberties Act of 1988. He returned to the position in 1999, and in the aftermath of 9/11, he once again mobilized his extensive press contacts and leveraged his political capital in the service of protecting civil rights. At this time, the diaspora that had scattered Japanese Americans across the country was now a boon to his efforts. Members of 113 separate JACL chapters were ready to go to work.

The day after the attack on the World Trade Center, Tateishi sent letters on behalf of the JACL to President George W. Bush and Attorney General John Ashcroft, exhorting them to not "make the same mistake" their predecessors had made in 1942. He also sent copies to JACL's regional offices, as well as press releases to "every major outlet."

John Tateishi, National Japanese American Memorial, Washington, D.C., 2013.

"Within half an hour, I started getting phone calls," Tateishi recalled. "What I really emphasized was that this is only the second time in the history of this country we were attacked on our own soil, [and] that in 1942 the government's response was to round up and imprison every Japanese American regardless of guilt or innocence and in total violation of the Constitution." But this time, thanks to the work of the CWRIC, and specifically to its publication of the report *Personal Justice Denied*, there was federally recognized evidence that "substantiated how terribly wrong that was and gave remedies to try to prevent it from happening again."

In Denver, fellow Manzanar survivor Rose Hanawa Tanaka, the wife of army veteran and urban planner Floyd Tanaka, also felt compelled to work with the Arab and Muslim communities against any kind of backlash. As a former public school teacher and retired social worker with Denver's Bureau of Public Welfare, Tanaka understood systemic inequality and racism, and she was ready to take a stand.

"When you see something like 9/11 happen, and the hatred that came up against Muslims in our country," Rose recalled, "we had [no choice but] to protect the Muslim women to go grocery shopping . . . [and] to form circles around their mosques." At every possible opportunity, Rose went on to tell her own story to students, reminding them, "You're the future of this country and the world . . . . It's not going to be perfect, but if we're going to have a true society that helps improve, we must all work on it."

In Detroit—where the country's largest Arab American population lived—Saburo Sasaki, who was held in Manzanar at seven years of age, was also speaking up. He had taken the first step when Iraqi coworkers were targeted ten years earlier during Operation Desert Storm. At the time, Sasaki had recently retired from a thirty-year career as an engineer for General Motors and was consulting with a friend who produced audio engineering equipment.

"I had two Iraqis working for me," Sasaki recalled, "and they were really antsy." He called a meeting and sought to reassure them that, "at least at work, they shouldn't feel this way." He told them about his own experiences during World War II and soon asked the local JACL office if he could join their speakers' bureau. "That Desert Storm experience, . . . that's what triggered it," he recalled. Throughout the 1990s and early 2000s, Saburo Sasaki shared his story with even wider audiences.

In 2004, he returned to Manzanar with his wife, Ann, to see the recently completed Visitor Center, inside the old high school auditorium at Manzanar. Almost every year since then, the Sasakis have returned to Manzanar to work as volunteer docents for the entire month of May. "I come back to talk to the students," Saburo reflected, "because I feel the students are the future . . . . By talking to them and letting them know what happened to us during World War II, they will [learn to] exercise their rights as they grow older and become full-fledged citizens, so that this type of thing will not happen again."

Manzanar survivor and volunteer park guide Saburo Sasaki speaks with a group of children in the reconstructed mess hall at Manzanar National Historic Site during the 47th Annual Manzanar Pilgrimage, April 2016.

"NO REDRESS"

Manzanar looms large in the collective history of Japanese Americans, but it is also part of the nation's larger history, and preserving the lessons of the camps is vital to ensuring such tragedies never happen again. Voicing Manzanar's message to people who may have no personal connection to it is central to the art and activism of poet traci kato-kiriyama, daughter of Manzanar survivors George and Iku Kiriyama. traci was in high school during Operation Desert Storm and felt moved to speak out when she heard people "referring to the camps in relation to 'rounding up Arab Americans' as an option our government should consider." She couldn't believe it then and was "astonished at the vehement increase of this sentiment after 9/11."

traci grew up attending Manzanar pilgrimages with her parents, who were both educators within the Los Angeles Unified School District. Her father, George, was also a member of the district's school board. "It was on the way to Manzanar," kato-kiriyama recalled, "that I vividly remember my parents instructing me to pay attention to the places they were taking me as a form of education. As the years passed and I stepped onto the grounds of Manzanar each year during pilgrimage, I also came to understand the connections we had to other communities—from the indigenous/Native American peoples . . . to . . . immigrants and migrant workers from Mexico and Central and South America, to the . . . institutional racism and oppression of black folks for the duration of this country."

In her poem "No Redress," she writes about her connection to Manzanar and its larger presence in modern society.

No Redress

no museum
no monument

no poem
no song
can house
the spirit
of a lost soul
like my Grandpa
who died before
the fruition
of justice could meet
the old man
at
his mailbox

Grandpa
never got to
stand in line
at the bank
with the pride
of redress check
in hand
one foot in front
of the other
feeling grounded again

never got to deposit
an apology
in
his savings account

never got to wonder
of how he might
spend
this money
on new equipment
for the nursery or
a truck for himself or
college money for
his grandchildren
or
for once
get the most
takai cuts
from the fish truck man

most years
in April

I attend
Pilgrimage

I say
Hello Manzanar

I bow at the graves

I speak to the wind
of my hopes
for
Afterlife
to be a real thing

not so I can see
Grandpa again

but for him
to look around today
to jump in the circle
to dance
the Tanko Bushi with me
and watch me get it right

and see our friends
all our relations
to learn what we mean by
    chosen family
we are all here

not only to remember

but to remind the local docents
this place will never
be a museum

and to leave Pilgrimage
with pledges as concrete
as the monument

we sing songs
to keep each other awake
on the long ride home

we lose sight quickly
rearview mirrors

a pitch black sky

where they close the gate
at the hour
they have had enough of us

where we leave behind
parts of our
best poetry

where I hope not
but
think
Grandpa
sits
still
waiting

PAST, PRESENT, AND FUTURE

Since Manzanar's Visitor Center opened in 2004, approximately one million people have visited the site. More than two thousand people attended the annual pilgrimage in 2017, the year of the seventy-fifth anniversary of E.O. 9066, and the event has stayed true to its grass-roots origins even while the host is now an agency of the same government that ordered the mass incarceration in the first place.

By venturing onto Manzanar's soil, visitors from all backgrounds can both touch the past and decide how to help shape the future. For some people, the journey back may be singular and fleeting, lasting only an hour or two. For others, the journey is a seasonal migration, playing out every spring and summer, sometimes for weeks or months at a time.

Many come to volunteer and share their stories with visitors, and it is through their efforts and the work of many others that Manzanar is being transformed yet again: a guard tower now looms over the

Mo Nishida, who was incarcerated in Colorado, prays at the Manzanar cemetery on the eve of the 47th Annual Manzanar Pilgrimage, April 2016.

landscape, ponds and gardens have been restored, and Block 14 once again has a mess hall, a women's latrine, barrack "apartments," a classroom, and a basketball court. National Park Service staff at Manzanar have worked closely with former incarcerees to create new exhibits and to re-create or restore original features that accurately represent life in the camp. As Chief of Interpretation Alisa Lynch explains, the fundamental goal of NPS staff is to help visitors "feel the era," to evoke a sense of the camp experience that is grounded in history.

••• ••• •••

On a bright summer day in 2008, four generations of Takayanagi family members gathered at Manzanar's cemetery to pay their respects.

At two and a half, the youngest was the same age as some of the kids in Manzanar's Children's Village who, sixty-five years earlier, had inspired Jack Takayanagi to vow he would do everything within his power to make sure this would never happen again.

This time, the child who sparked his dream for the future was his own great-granddaughter, Kayli.

As she played in the light and shadow that is particular to Manzanar's high desert landscape, the elder Takayanagi, now in his eighties, reflected: "I pray and hope that for Kayli this will always be a historic place, nothing else."

MAKING DESERTS BLOOM

Manzanar National Historic Site welcomed 105,307 visitors in 2016, and its message has spread to many more individuals and communities throughout the world. As part of an international coalition of "sites of conscience" whose purpose is to preserve, interpret, and chronicle painful chapters in human history, the evocative nature of the visitor experience at Manzanar is consistent with this larger purpose of the International Coalition of Sites of Conscience. "By stepping in the shoes of those who have struggled before us," writes Elizabeth Silkes, director of the organization, "we not only see how far we still have to go, but also begin to determine exactly how to get there."

Karyl Matsumoto returns to the grounds near Manzanar's Children's Village, April 2016. Karyl was an infant when she first arrived at Manzanar in 1943; she had been transferred there from Tule Lake, where she had been born to an unwed mother. When Lillian Matsumoto, who ran the orphanage at Manzanar with her husband, Harry, first met Karyl, she remembered thinking: "She looked like she had a lot of souls . . . . Though she was only three and a half months [old], she just put her hands [up] and she grabbed one of my fingers." Lillian and Harry adopted Karyl as they prepared to leave Manzanar, later settling in Berkeley, California, where they raised a family that expanded to include their son Kent. Karyl entered politics in 1997 and served as mayor and council member for the City of South San Francisco for most of her professional life.

Above: Rena Ogino, a student at the University of California, San Diego, speaks to the crowd at the 47th Annual Manzanar Pilgrimage, April 2016.

Below: Saburo Sasaki, only seven years old when he arrived at Manzanar, discusses his wartime experiences with visitors in the reconstructed mess hall, April 2016.

In the case of Hank Umemoto, the path to reclaiming Manzanar started when he was fourteen years old, coming of age behind barbed wire. As dusk turned to darkness one night in camp, he glimpsed from his barracks window "two eerie, faint flickering lights" descending the mountain and sending shivers down his spine. In the fading light, he saw car lights coming down the road from Mount Whitney, the tallest peak in the contiguous United States. Hank vowed to summit the peak when he was "a free man again." Fifty-seven years—and one failed attempt—later, he kept his vow, and would go on to summit Mount Whitney nine more times.

As he chased his aging hiker's dream of conquering "the Big One," Umemoto took another quixotic stand: he rejected monetary reparations from the U.S. government because he didn't want to be "considered a victim of injustice." In his written response to the U.S. Department of Justice, he asserted his "claim" on Manzanar and how he felt its story should be told: "I claim this former desert community, for it is so much a part of me." When in need of solace, he would often return to "what used to be Manzanar," and would soon feel "well and confident again," in part because he was reminded of "those diligent

Reconstructed guard tower at Manzanar, 2016.

Issei and Nisei, who with pride and determination faced that wartime episode . . . and ventured into totally unfamiliar and often hostile communities to start their lives from 'square one.'"

Umemoto's desire to honor this resilience led him to become a docent at Manzanar in 2006 and to join archeological dig teams led by the National Park Service. "With each excavation," Umemoto wrote, "we are reaffirming the resilience of Manzanar's residents—people who turned their prison into a productive community, where they worked and played and patiently dreamt of better days to come amid the serenity and beauty of gardens and ponds with cascading waterfalls and carp swirling in the waters under black locust trees."

The jewel of these gardens was first called Rose Park and then Pleasure Park before it was renamed to recognize Manzanar's project director Ralph P. Merritt. During the war, what began as a Western-style rose garden evolved into a nearly two-acre park that included ponds, streams, and a Japanese-style strolling garden. It was an oasis, affording the only vistas in camp that weren't marred by barracks, guard towers, and barbed wire. Ralph Merritt once hoped it would become a permanent fixture and tourist destination within Owens Valley. Now, decades later and with the help of descendants of garden designer and expert rose cultivator Kuichiro Nishi (whose granddaughter Karen Ishizuka curated the JANM exhibition "America's Concentration Camps" in 1994), Merritt Park

Henry Nishi rebuilding his father's bridge, 2011.

is indeed blooming again. Led by National Park Service archaeologist Jeff Burton, Manzanar survivor Henry Nishi (Kuichiro Nishi's son and Karen's uncle) has teamed up with family members to reconstruct two wooden bridges and other features of the park.

The ties to Manzanar are personal as well as professional for NPS preservation specialist and certified arborist David Goto. His great-uncle was Dr. James Goto, the onetime director of Manzanar's hospital; his wife's family has roots in the Owens Valley dating to the late 1800s; and he is now charged with restoring and maintaining Manzanar's gardens, ponds, basketball courts, and hand-dug cellars. He approaches these projects with insights gained as the recipient of a 2016 Aurora Challenge Grant, which he used to attend a garden workshop in Sendai, Japan, one of the communities hardest hit by the 2011 tsunami. Along with participants from around the world, Goto helped build a garden "to console and commemorate the victims" of the tsunami. "Just as Manzanar's prisoners built gardens to make something positive after the loss of their businesses, homes, and freedom," Goto wrote, "workshop participants [built] a garden to console the victims of the tsunami who lost everything they owned during the

David Goto at Manzanar, 2017.

2011 disaster." Goto not only left some of Manzanar's influence in a memorial garden in Sendai, but he also returned to Manzanar with a deeper appreciation for Japanese culture and with hands-on knowledge of the techniques and tools that Issei gardeners would have used there in the 1940s.

The same year Hank Umemoto had made his unsuccessful attempt to summit Mount Whitney, Henry Fukuhara, a Manzanar survivor, retired florist, and watercolorist, invited a group of artists and art students to gather in the peak's foothills for lessons in plein air painting. Fukuhara would go on to lead more than a dozen "Manzanar Paint Outs" between 1998 and 2008. Paintings from the workshops were exhibited in Manzanar's Visitor Center and in galleries throughout Southern California each year, increasing awareness of wartime incarceration.

"When I paint at Manzanar I can't help remembering some aspect of life when I was here . . . with my family," Fukuhara wrote. "But I really don't dwell on that. I focus on making a painting, identifying the simple shapes that can serve as symbols of the place—the gate

Henry Fukuhara leads his eighth annual watercolor workshop at Manzanar, April 2005.

houses at the entrance, the monument in the cemetery, the guard towers, and the Sierras in the background . . . . It is up to the viewer to complete the process by responding to the painting."

Despite Fukuhara's insistence that his lessons were more about artistic composition than historic commentary, fellow artist and regular Paint Out participant Mary Higuchi credited these journeys with lifting the veil on her own family's history. Higuchi and her family were sent to camp in Poston, Arizona, yet she said the subject was never a topic of conversation within the family. Those Manzanar Paint Outs, she said, had "recently stimulated conversation with my mother about her experiences."

By contrast, artist Momo Nagano rarely shied away from discussing her wartime experiences with her children. She also freely credited her time spent weaving in Manzanar's camouflage net factory as a source of inspiration for her work as a textile artist later in life. "Through her stories," recalls her son Dan Kwong, "Manzanar became a defining

Above left: Momo Nagano at work, c. 1975.

Above right: Textile artist Momo Nagano's *American Families*—shown here on display at the Japanese American National Museum in November 2010—is a flag inscribed with the names of the camps and of families from her prewar neighborhood, the Seinan district southwest of downtown Los Angeles.

experience in terms of understanding the depth of anti-Asian racism in American society, the flaws of governmental leadership, and the effects of internalized racism."

In 1972, the year that Manzanar received designation as a state historical landmark, Karl and Elaine Black Yoneda took part in the annual pilgrimage. Thirty years after Karl left Manzanar to volunteer for military service, the veteran, union organizer, and activist reflected on Manzanar's larger meaning in American history: "Manzanar is everywhere, whenever injustice raises its ugly head. It is in the Indian reservations with close to one million Native Americans still contained in them; it is in the ghettoes where thousands upon thousands of racial minorities are shunted; it is in the prisons where thousands are confined because most of them are poor and of different color and race."

Arthur Ogami also started attending the pilgrimages in the 1970s. He had been a prisoner at Manzanar before being sent to Tule Lake, and in 1945 he accompanied his family to Japan as a renunciant. He came back home with his Japanese wife, Kimiko, as a repatriated U.S. citizen in 1953.

Arthur Ogami chose to become a docent at Manzanar after he retired from his work as an electronics repairman. "I'm here to tell my side of how things happened," he told a reporter at the 42nd annual pilgrimage. And park visitors aren't the only ones who have benefited from Arthur's willingness to share his story; his own son, Gene, learns something new each time. "Growing up, my dad never really talked about life in Manzanar," said the younger Ogami. "But every time we visit here, I find out something new about his experience."

When Ben Ogami, Arthur Ogami's brother, reconnected with his friend Gordon Sato at the Manzanar High School Reunion in 1984, the unlikely pair did not know it was the beginning of an effort that would change many lives. After meeting at Manzanar as teenagers, they lost touch when they went their separate ways and the Ogami family moved to Japan. Ben regained his citizenship only after "losing ten years in Japan," while Gordon, who had started a vegetable garden at Manzanar as a teenager, went on to a celebrated career as a cell biologist and co-inventor of a cancer treatment drug.

In the 1980s, Sato devoted himself to philanthropy and plowed a portion of his pharmaceutical company royalties into an agricultural project designed to aid war-torn communities in Eritrea, bordering the Red Sea in East Africa. His vision: "Make a coastal village self-sufficient in food." Working with low-cost, low-tech materials—such as recycled nails as a supplementary iron source—Sato partnered with local people to plant hundreds of thousands of mangrove trees in coastal communities. These saltwater-tolerant trees provide habitat for fish, while their seeds and leaves provide livestock feed.

Sato dubbed his program the Manzanar Project. "I'm trying to make Manzanar into something good," he said of his quest. While the camp was not "as bad as Auschwitz," Sato asserted, "it was bad."

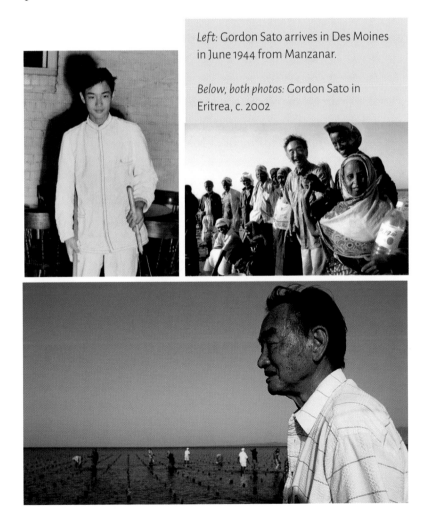

Left: Gordon Sato arrives in Des Moines in June 1944 from Manzanar.

Below, both photos: Gordon Sato in Eritrea, c. 2002

Ben Ogami, now reunited with his old friend, trekked to Eritrea with Sato as a volunteer in the mid-1980s and chose to make the country his new home. He helped green a desert with over a million mangrove trees while Sato, meanwhile, replicated his project in Mauritania in West Africa. Sato made frequent trips between his home in the United States and his Manzanar Project locations in East and West Africa. He died at age eighty-nine at his home in Massachusetts in 2017.

This far-flung work by Manzanar's survivors and their descendants, as well as by park staff and volunteer groups, continues to shape the meaning of Manzanar as a site of conscience—both within its original dusty footprint and in unexpected parts of the globe.

"NO MORE MANZANARS"

To a large degree, Shigetoshi Tateishi's admonition to his own children—"Don't ever forget this place"—has been secured for future generations by the establishment of Manzanar as a national historic site. Visitors to Manzanar have a chance to walk in the footsteps of Tateishi and the many thousands of others who were thrown together there after being yanked from their business districts in Los Angeles and San Francisco, their fishing towns in San Pedro, their truck farms in Southern and Central California's rich agricultural valleys, and their strawberry fields on Bainbridge Island in Washington State. But many visitors may leave Manzanar with unanswered questions about the "10,000 lives, 10,000 stories" that the park is dedicated to preserving.

Where did all the people go after the gates shut with a clang behind them? How did they pick up the pieces? What hurdles did they face outside the wire?

Some, like Shinjo Nagatomi and Sangoro Mayeda in Southern California, and Jack Takayanagi in New York and Oregon, responded by ministering to their traumatized communities in temples and churches and through social service agencies. Others, like Rose

Sean Miura, the grandson of Manzanar incarceree Paul Bannai, at the Women's March, Los Angeles, January 21, 2017.

Tanaka and Saburo Sasaki, ventured far from their West Coast homes to contribute to their new communities as social workers, teachers, engineers, and managers, sometimes becoming among the first to speak out against racial profiling in the wake of the Persian Gulf wars and the terrorist attacks of 9/11. For a notable few, like Joe Kurihara and Ernest Wakayama, dissent proved to be the only way to advocate for the democratic values they had so highly prized as U.S. citizens and veterans of World War I.

Still others, like Shigetoshi Tateishi and Kiyoshi Nishio, struggled to overcome the financial losses and psychological scars that their incarceration had caused, yet they nevertheless managed to pass the torch to members of the next generation—including their own sons, John and Alan, respectively—who became steadfast champions of redress and reparation. Through grassroots organizing, legal activism, and persistent research, people such as Sue Kunitomi Embrey, William Hohri, Aiko Herzig-Yoshinaga, and others defied Nisei stereotypes, pursued justice, and altered the course of history.

Although each of Manzanar's ten-thousand-plus souls left imprints on the dusty soil at the foot of Mount Williamson in California's Owens Valley, they left even deeper imprints on the American cultural and political landscape after they left Manzanar's confines. Through the alchemy of the human spirit and the resilience of the human soul, a group of people who were wrongfully imprisoned by their own government managed to reclaim and redefine their own personal, cultural, political, and artistic identities and assert in ways both private and public that there would be "no more Manzanars."

Above: Visitors listen to recordings about life inside the barracks during a tour of Manzanar National Historic Site during the 47th Annual Manzanar Pilgrimage, April 2016.

Below: Amara Munir explores the mess hall exhibits at Manzanar National Historic Site during the 47th Annual Manzanar Pilgrimage, April 2016.

In the wake of the seventy-fifth anniversary of the signing of E.O. 9066 by President Franklin D. Roosevelt and the 2017 signing of several refugee and travel bans by President Donald J. Trump, Sean Miura—an artist, a writer, and the grandson of World War II veteran and California assemblyman Paul Bannai—reflected: "The literal connections between the camps and today's political climate have been taught to me my whole life. It's the more subtle connections that I want to continue teasing out. What does it mean to survive in America during the twenty-first century? . . . What is the trauma of immigrating to America in the twenty-first century? What are the hopes and walls that second-generation children face today? We have these answers within us. How can we undo these generations of barbed wire between our teeth and question the refuge we so often find in silence?"

Little Tokyo hosted a vigil against Islamophobia, December 10, 2015.

AFTERWORD

As *Life after Manzanar* is built upon personal stories from those who experienced the camp firsthand, the main foundation of this book is the numerous oral history interviews that have been collected over the years since the war ended and the camps closed. With many voices come many perspectives and interpretations, and in some cases the narratives that emerge tell radically different stories about life post-Manzanar. It is with this knowledge that we have attempted to represent a wide range of experiences rather than try to create a single narrative about an entire population. Also, since individuals' memories can change over time, we have attempted to verify facts through crosschecking with official government documents and academic sources. Research materials gathered for the Visitor Center and other related exhibits at Manzanar National Historic Site were also used in the writing of this book. We also had email exchanges with a number of our subjects. For those who are inspired to learn more about the experience of Japanese Americans during World War II and in the decades that followed, we invite you to look deeper into the oral histories collected by, among others, Manzanar National Historic Site, Densho, the Japanese American National Museum, and California State University, Fullerton.

The late James Howell, who served as our main researcher, meticulously collected oral histories and related articles for us. Art Hansen, instrumental in the preservation of camp history, and Patricia Biggs, one of the rangers at Manzanar National Historic Site, vetted the manuscript, pointing out when we came to perhaps incorrect or questionable conclusions. Gayle Wattawa, overseer of this project, and copyeditor Lisa K. Marietta, both of Heyday, provided guidance and meticulous editorial notes to improve the text. We are indebted to them all for their comments and we take full responsibility for the final product. We don't purport that *Life after Manzanar* is a definitive or exhaustive history of Japanese Americans after the World War II camp experience, and we know and expect that scholars will continue to unearth new information and statistics about the little-known resettlement period. We look forward to learning more about this important time in our nation's history.

One of the initiators of this project, the late Maggie Wittenburg, wanted *Life after Manzanar* to reach the average visitor to Manzanar National Historic Site who might wonder what happened to people after they left the barracks for the great unknown. We want to honor Maggie's vision for the project, and we hope we have done so through the voices and personal experiences of the individuals featured in this book.

Naomi Hirahara and
Heather Lindquist

BIBLIOGRAPHY

ORAL HISTORIES

Conducted for *Life after Manzanar* by Naomi Hirahara and Heather Lindquist
Sumiko "Sumi" Azeka Funo (telephone interview, September 16, 2016)
David Goto (telephone interview, February 6, 2017)
Iku Kato Kiriyama (May 17, 2016)
Alan Takeshi Nishio (February 5, 2016)
Shirley Nagatomi Okabe (various telephone and mail correspondence, 2016)

From Manzanar National Historic Site
Sue Kunitomi Embrey (Signature Productions[1])
Henry Fukuhara (Signature Productions)
Henry and Fujiko Fukuhara (June 21, 2002)
Jeanne Wakatsuki Houston (August 29, 2014)
George Izumi (November 6, 2002)
Bill Michael (July 29, 1999)
Robert Miyatake (February 7, 2016)
Victor Muraoka (October 18, 2006)
Henry Nishi (January 8, 2009, and April 8, 2009)
Mary Kageyama Nomura (November 7, 2002)
Mary Kageyama Nomura (Signature Productions)
Ben Ogami (October 15, 2008)
Shirley Nagatomi Okabe (January 30, 2013)
Jack Takayanagi (April 22, 2008)
Rose Hanawa Tanaka (August 9, 2011)
John Tateishi (November 7, 2013)

From Densho
Lorraine Bannai (March 23–24, 2000)
Fumiko Hayashida (March 16, 1998)

---

1. Signature Productions conducted targeted oral history interviews for the film "Remembering Manzanar," which runs every half hour at Manzanar National Historic Site.

Aiko Herzig-Yoshinaga (September 11, 1997)
William Hohri (September 12, 1997)
George Izumi (November 6, 2002)
Mary Kageyama Nomura (July 9, 2009)
Bruce Kaji (July 28, 2010)
Roy Murakami (January 8, 2009)
Henry Nishi (January 8, 2009)
Grace Shinoda Nakamura (January 25, 2012)
Shirley Nagatomi Okabe (January 30, 2013)
Jack Takayanagi (August 22, 2008)
Hank Umemoto (July 30, 2010)

From California State University, Fullerton/Japanese American Oral History
Project
Sue Kunitomi Embrey (August 24, 1973, and November 15, 1973)
Togo Tanaka (August 30, 1973)
Karl Yoneda (March 2, 1974)

From the Japanese American National Museum/Regenerations Oral History
Project
Aiko Herzig-Yoshinaga (August 26, 1988)
William Hohri (June 12, 1998)
Jeanne Wakatsuki Houston (December 27, 2005)
Mary Nishi Ishizuka (May 27, 1998)
Togo Tanaka (December 18, 1997)

From the California State Archives State Government Oral History Program
Paul Bannai (March 8 and 20, 1989)

From the National Coalition for Redress and Reparations
Alan Nishio (May 27, 2014)

From the Japanese American Medical Association
Masako Kusayanagi Miura (July 26, 2002)
Mary Sakaguchi Oda (August 15, 2002)
Sanbo Sakaguchi (August 14, 2002)

From California State University, Long Beach
Alan Nishio (October 1, 1993)

From *The Idaho Homefront: Of Camps and Combat* (2007; documentary by Alberto Moreno)
Fumiko Hayashida

From *Three Lenses: Born Free and Equal* (2015; documentary by Ecar Oden)
Edgar Wakayama
John Tateishi

From the Seabrook Education Center
Charles Nagao (April 1, 1986)

From the University of Massachusetts, Boston (*From Confinement to College: Video Oral Histories of Japanese American Students in World War II*)
Gordon Sato (February 3, 2011)

From the University of Washington/University Libraries' Oral History Collection
Karl Yoneda (January 26, 1984)

From the University of California, Berkeley/Japanese American Women Collection
Lillian Iida Matsumoto (February 2, 2008)

CHAPTER ONE

There are limited volumes of academic literature about the resettlement of Japanese Americans after they were released from camp during and immediately following World War II. Greg Robinson, a professor at l'Université du Québec à Montréal, broke new ground with *After Camp: Portraits in Midcentury Japanese American Life and Politics* (Berkeley: University of California Press, 2012), but otherwise, the early resettlement story has been preserved mostly through personal memoirs and more narrowly focused papers or books. The book *Nanka Nikkei Voices: Resettlement Years, 1945–1955*, edited by Brian Niiya and produced by the now defunct Japanese American Historical Society of Southern California in 1998, was one of the first attempts to collect essays from former incarcerees. Pieces included in that volume by Hank Umemoto, Iku Kato Kiriyama, Art Takemoto, and Victor Muraoka were specifically helpful in the writing of this book. Niiya has also written extensively for Densho, and his entry on the Densho website about resettlement and wartime hostels is probably the most comprehensive piece on this topic. Muraoka has also elaborated on his experiences in an unpublished memoir written for his family, "When I Was Your Age...," and Umemoto wrote a book, *Manzanar to Mount Whitney: The Life and Times of a Lost Hiker*, which was published by Heyday in 2013.

Books about the wider experience of incarcerees include *Making Home from War* (Heyday, 2011), edited by Brian Komei Dempster (it does not include reminiscences by any Manzanar incarcerees but is another fine anthology of memoirs) and Charlotte Brooks's *Alien Neighbors, Foreign Friends: Asian Americans, Housing, and the Transformation of Urban California* (Chicago: University of Chicago Press, 2009), which places the return of Japanese Americans to California in a larger context. For information on Little Tokyo, there are Scott Kurashige's excellent book *The Shifting Grounds of Race: Black and Japanese Americans in the Making of Multiethnic Los Angeles* (Princeton, NJ: Princeton University Press, 2008) and Lon Kurashige's compelling and comprehensive *Japanese American Celebration and Conflict: A History of Ethnic Identity and Festival in Los Angeles, 1934–1990* (Berkeley: University of California Press, 2002). The website produced by Martha Nakagawa on Bronzeville (http://bronzeville-la.ltsc.org/) features various photographs of historical importance, and an unpublished article by Michihiro Ama of the University of Alaska, "A Multiracial Buddhist Lawsuit in Postwar Los Angeles," includes never-before-revealed details about the rental of the Nishi Hongwanji temple during World War II.

For information about the situation in Los Angeles, the daily reports written by Tom Sasaki, a field worker for the Bureau of Sociological Research at Poston and for the War Agency Liquidation Unit in Los Angeles, were invaluable. Details included in this book were distilled from reports he filed from July 24, 1946, to August 28, 1946. Information about "California incidents of terrorism"—specifically violence directed at Japanese Americans who had resettled on the West Coast—were found in a confidential memo written to WRA director Dillon S. Myer by M. M. Tozier, chief of reports for the WRA.

WRA and American Field Service Committee reports are rich in detail and little-known observations. Chicago came alive through both Togo Tanaka's documentary reports in 1943 and WRA analyst John Edward de Young's documentation (the latter accessed through the Japanese American Evacuation and Resettlement Digital Archive at UC Berkeley). Primary source documents about the Chicago Resettlers Committee are maintained by the Japanese American Service Committee's online Legacy Center Archives and Library.

Certain biographical accounts were extremely helpful in developing the personal stories of some of the individuals featured in the book. Jeanne Wakatsuki Houston and James Houston's groundbreaking book, *Farewell to Manzanar*, includes information about her family's resettlement to Cabrillo Homes in Long Beach, and Diana Meyers Bahr's *The Unquiet Nisei: An Oral History of the Life of Sue Kunitomi Embrey* has wonderful information especially about Embrey's courtship and marriage. Frank Chuman published his memoir, *Manzanar and Beyond*, with the Asian American Curriculum Project in San Mateo in 2011.

Catherine Irwin's *Twice Orphaned: Voices from the Children's Village of Manzanar* (Fullerton, CA: Center for Oral and Public History, California State University, Fullerton, 2008) is the definitive work on the camp orphanage. "Invisible Restraints: Life and Labor at Seabrook Farms" (http://www.njdigitalhighway.org/exhibits/seabrook_farms/exhibit.php) is a very fine digital exhibition that was curated by undergraduate and graduate students enrolled in the Rutgers University course "Public Histories of Detention and Mass Incarceration" in fall of 2015. James Howell also spoke to Pauline Nagao Culk and Irene Kaneshiki, the twin daughters of Charles and Mary Nagao, in telephone conversations on March 17, 2016, and March 18, 2016, respectively.

Other Sources

"Burbank Citizens Fight Nisei's Use of Barracks." *Los Angeles Times*, September 28, 1945.

Burton, Jeffrey F. *Three Farewells to Manzanar: The Archeology of Manzanar National Historic Site, California.* Tucson: Western Archeological and Conservation Center, National Park Service, U.S. Department of the Interior, 1996.

Copeland, Jeffrey C. "Stay for a Dollar a Day: California's Church Hostels and Support during the Japanese American Eviction and Resettlement, 1942–1947." M.A. thesis, University of Nevada, Reno, 2014.

Esaki, John, prod. and dir. *Words, Weavings, and Songs.* Video. Japanese American National Museum, 2002.

Harrison, C. H. *Growing a Global Village: Making History at Seabrook Farms.* New York: Holmes and Meier, 2003.

"Help Sought for Japs at Camp in Burbank." *Los Angeles Times*, May 15, 1946.

Hirabayashi, Lane Ryo. *Japanese American Resettlement Through the Lens.* Boulder: University Press of Colorado, 2009.

Hirahara, Naomi, and Gwenn M. Jensen. *Silent Scars of Healing Hands: Oral Histories of Japanese American Doctors in World War II Detention Camps.* Fullerton, CA: Center for Oral and Public History, California State University, Fullerton, 2004.

"Housing 513 Japs Creates Problem." *Los Angeles Times*, May 13, 1946.

"Jap Returnees Take Over Burbank Barracks." *Los Angeles Times*, November 6, 1945.

"Jap-Americans, Veterans' Kin, Live in Trailers." *Los Angeles Times*, November 9, 1945.

Kashima, Tetsuden. *Judgment without Trial: Japanese-American Imprisonment during World War II.* Seattle: University of Washington Press, 2003.

Kwong, Dan, prod. and dir. *Momo's Excellent Adventure.* Video. 2015.

Little Tokyo Historical Society. *Los Angeles's Little Tokyo.* Charleston, SC: Arcadia Publishing, 2010.

Marchevsky, Alejandra, and Jeanne Theoharis. *Not Working: Latina Immigrants, Low-wage Jobs, and the Failure of Welfare Reform.* New York: New York University Press, 2006.

Myer, Dillon S. *Uprooted Americans: The Japanese Americans and the War Relocation Authority during World War II.* Tucson: University of Arizona Press, 1971.

"Official Row Flares Up Over Freed Japs' Return." *Los Angeles Times,* January 13, 1945.

Omoto, Sada. "Felix Norte in Visit to Friends at Manzanar." *Bainbridge Island Review,* October 15, 1942.

"Pact Paves Way for Japs' Return." *Los Angeles Times,* October 20, 1945.

Russell, Jan Jarboe. *The Train to Crystal City: FDR's Secret Prisoner Exchange Program and America's Only Family Internment Camp during World War II.* New York: Scribner, 2015.

Sawada, Mitziko. "After the Camps: Seabrook Farms, New Jersey, and the Resettlement of Japanese Americans, 1944–47." *Amerasia Journal* 13, no. 2 (1986–87): 117–36.

Seabrook, John. "The Spinach King." *New Yorker,* February 20, 1995.

Smothers, Ronald. "A New Chapter for a Village, Once Barracks." *New York Times* (Upper Deerfield Journal), October 4, 2006.

Thomas, Dorothy S., and Richard Nishimoto. *The Spoilage: Japanese-American Evacuation and Resettlement During World War II.* Berkeley: University of California Press, 1946.

Tsukashima, Ronald Tadao. "Politics of Maintenance Gardening and the Formation of the Southern California Gardeners' Federation." In *Green Makers: Japanese American Gardeners in Southern California,* by Naomi Hirahara. Los Angeles: Southern California Gardeners' Federation, 2000.

Umemoto, Hank. Letter to the National Park Service c/o Kara Miyagishima, November 5, 2014.

Woo, Elaine. "Rev. Julius Goldwater; Convert to Buddhism Aided WWII Internees." *Los Angeles Times,* June 23, 2001.

CHAPTER TWO

Hillary Jenks's 2014 article "Seasoned Long Enough in Concentration: Suburbanization and Transnational Citizenship in Southern California's South Bay" (*Journal of Urban History* 40, no. 1) was especially illuminating on the subject of the many former incarcerees who returned to or resettled in Gardena. Christina Klein's *Cold War Orientalism: Asia in the Middlebrow Imagination, 1945–1961* (Berkeley: University of California Press, 2003) and Ellen D. Wu's *The Color of Success: Asian Americans and the Origins of the Model Minority* (Princeton, NJ: Princeton University Press, 2014) both introduced new interpretations of the post–World War II period, and Wu's work informed this book's passages on both the Nikkei Progressives and the role of Nisei veterans in the mainstream acceptance of Japanese Americans during the postwar era.

In Defense of Justice: Joseph Kurihara and the Japanese American Struggle for Equality (Chicago: University of Illinois Press, 2013), by Eileen H. Tamura, was essential in our writing about this remarkable dissident leader. Kurihara's papers are also available at UC Berkeley's Bancroft Library as part of the Japanese Relocation Papers.

Jeffrey F. Burton's *Garden Management Plan: Gardens and Gardeners at Manzanar*, produced for the National Park Service in 2015, is a wealth of information on those who beautified the landscape of Manzanar, including Kuichiro Nishi.

Dennis Reed, a photography professor, was the curator of the Japanese American National Museum's exhibition "Making Waves: Japanese American Photography, 1920–1940," which ran from February 28 to June 26, 2016. He kindly provided a statement on the work of Toyo Miyatake.

Iku Kato Kiriyama also shared with us correspondence written by her brother, Roy.

Other Sources

Benford, Tom. "Larry Shinoda's Last Interview." *Vette*, December 1997.

Chuman, Dwight. "Memories of a Pilgrimage Gone By." *Rafu Shimpo*, April 19, 1975.

Chuman, Frank F. *The Bamboo People: The Law and Japanese-Americans*. Del Mar, CA: Publisher's, Inc., 1976.

Hawaii Nikkei History Editorial Board. *Japanese Eyes, American Heart: Personal Reflections of Hawaii's World War II Nisei Soldiers*. Honolulu: Tendai Educational Foundation, 1988.

Houston, James D., and Jeanne Wakatsuki Houston. "One Can Think About Life After the Fish Is in the Canoe & Beyond Manzanar: Views of Asian-American Womanhood." Santa Barbara: Capra Press, 1985.

Kado, Ryozo. Memoir dictated to Maryknoll nun, 1964. Available at Maryknoll Mission Archives, Maryknoll, New York.

Kaji, Bruce T., with Sharon Yamato. *Jive Bomber: A Sentimental Journey*. Gardena, CA: Kaji and Associates, 2010.

Miyatake, Toyo. *Miyatake Toyo no Shashin: Toyo Miyatake Behind the Camera, 1923–1979*. Tokyo: Bungei Shunju, 1984.

Raineri, Vivian McGukin. *The Red Angel: The Life and Times of Elaine Black Yoneda, 1906–1988*. New York: International Publishers, 1991.

Takamoto, Iwao, with Michael Mallory. *Iwao Takamoto: My Life with a Thousand Characters*. Jackson: University Press of Mississippi, 2009.

Taylor, Frank J. "Wizard with Rocks." *Saturday Evening Post*, August 5, 1961.

Yoneda, Karl. *Ganbatte: Sixty-Year Struggle of a Kibei Worker*. Los Angeles: UCLA Asian American Studies Center, 1984.

CHAPTER THREE

The full transcripts from the Commission on Wartime Relocation and Internment of Civilians are available from many sources, including online through the Los Angeles County library system. The testimonies used for this chapters were from the following individuals: Frank Chuman (August 4, 1981, Los Angeles), Sue Kunitomi Embrey (August 5, 1981, Los Angeles), William Hohri (July 16, 1981, Washington, D.C.), Hannah Holmes (August 4, 1981, Los Angeles), Mary Ishizuka (August 5, 1981, Los Angeles), Jim Kawaminami (August 5, 1981, Los Angeles), Charles Nagao (November 23, 1981, New York), Alan Nishio (August 4, 1981, Los Angeles), and Ernest Kinzo Wakayama (August 11, 1981, San Francisco). Shigeko Kitamoto's written testimony was submitted for the hearings in Seattle, Washington, September 9–11, 1981.

Karen L. Ishizuka's *Lost and Found: Reclaiming the Japanese American Incarceration* (Urbana: University of Illinois Press, 2006) is a wonderful documentation of the Japanese American National Museum's exhibition "America's Concentration Camps." Ishizuka also more recently published *Serve the People: Making Asian America in the Long Sixties* (London: Verso, 2016). Another good resource on political mobilization and consciousness in the 1960s is *Asian Americans: The Movement and the Moment*, edited by Steve Louie and Glenn Omatsu and published by the UCLA Asian American Studies Center Press (2001).

We also exchanged email correspondence with Kathryn and Lorraine Bannai in January and February 2017.

Other Sources

Bannai, Kathryn. "Gordon Hirabayashi v. United States: 'This is an American case.'" *Seattle Journal for Social Justice* 11, no. 1 (2012): article 4.

Bannai, Lorraine. *Enduring Conviction: Fred Korematsu and His Quest for Justice.* Seattle: University of Washington Press, 2015.

Culver, Virginia. "Urban Planner Said Little of WWII Camp, Service." *Denver Post*, February 19, 2008.

Curtis, Mary. "Arson-Plagued Church Revived." *Los Angeles Times*, July 8, 1982.

De Leonardis, Anthony. "The Lively Early Years of U.S. Judo." *Black Belt*, March 1967.

"DU Opened Doors to Japanese-Americans Imprisoned during WWII." *University of Denver Magazine*, June 23, 2008.

Friedson, Anthony. "No More Farewells: An Interview with Jeanne and John Houston." *Biography* 7, no. 1 (Winter 1984).

Gardena Buddhist Church booklet published for its fiftieth anniversary, 1976.

Hirabayashi, Lane Ryo. "Community Lost? Notes on the Significance of a Contemporary Japanese American Community in Southern California." In *Asians in America: A Reader*, edited by Malcolm Collier. Dubuque, IA: Kendall-Hunt, 1993.

Hohri, William Minoru. *Repairing America: An Account of the Movement for Japanese-American Redress.* Pullman: Washington State University Press, 1988.

———. *Resistance: Challenging America's Wartime Internment of Japanese-Americans.* Lomita, CA: The Epistolarian, 2001.

Keller, Helen. Letter to Hannah Holmes, August 3, 1943. Courtesy of Dwight Holmes.

Maeda, Daryl Joji. *Rethinking the Asian American Movement.* New York: Routledge, 2012.

Maki, Mitchell T., Harry H. L. Kitano, and S. Megan Berhold. *Achieving the Impossible Dream: How Japanese Americans Obtained Redress.* Urbana: University of Illinois Press, 1999.

Moran, Julio. "Court Rules Accused Arsonist Insane." *Los Angeles Times*, November 24, 1983.

Tateishi, John. *And Justice for All: An Oral History of the Japanese American Detention Camps.* New York: Random House, 1984.

Willis, Jennifer. "NW Love Stories: Jack and Mary Takayanagi Share 71 Years of Love and Marriage." *The Oregonian*, January 2, 2015.

CHAPTER FOUR

Jeanne Wakatsuki Houston masterfully tells of her experience visiting Manzanar National Historic Site with her daughter Cori in her essay "Crossing Boundaries," in *The Colors of Nature: Culture, Identity, and the Natural World*, edited by Alison Hawthorne Deming and Lauret E. Savoy (2011).

Satsuki Ina, renowned in the subject of generational trauma, produced a documentary on this topic, *Children of the Camps*, and delivered the keynote speech at the Manzanar pilgrimage in 2015; the transcript of her speech, as well as those of other honorees, can be found online at the Manzanar Committee's website, www.manzanarcommittee.org.

Robert T. Hayashi's article "Transfigured Patterns: Contesting Memories at the Manzanar National Historic Site," published in the fall 2003 issue of *The Public Historian*, deftly touches upon how Manzanar continues to affect the psyches of both former incarcerees and others.

John Tateishi's account of responding to 9/11 is documented in a profile written by Deanne Stone in the September 2014 issue of "OLLI Outlook," the newsletter of the Osher Lifelong Learning Institute at the University of California, Berkeley.

William Booth's "A Lonely Patch of History," published in the *Washington Post* (April 15, 1997), describes the Manzanar site as being neglected in the mid-1990s.

We also exchanged email correspondence with traci-kato kiriyama and Sean Miura.

EPILOGUE

Henry Fukuhara Paint Out Collection, 1992–2011. California State University, Dominquez Hills, Special Collections.

Ladino, Jennifer K. "Mountains, Monuments, and Other Matter: Environmental Affects at Manzanar." *Environmental Humanities* 6 (2015).

The Manzanar Project website, http://themanzanarproject.com.

Pollack, Andrew. "A Drug's Royalties May Ease Hunger." *New York Times*, March 17, 2004.

IMAGE CREDITS

Frontispiece (p. ii): Toyo Miyatake Studio
Pages vi and vii: Toyo Miyatake Studio

Chapter One

Facing page 1: Toyo Miyatake Studio
Page 2: Courtesy of Shirley Nagatomi Okabe
Page 3: Toyo Miyatake Studio
Page 4, top: Nagatomi Family Collection, Manzanar National Historic Site
Page 4, bottom: Courtesy of Shirley Nagatomi Okabe
Page 7, all photos: Center for Oral and Public History, California State University, Fullerton
Page 8: The Bancroft Library, University of California, Berkeley
Page 9: Toyo Miyatake Studio
Page 11, top: Courtesy of Manzanar National Historic Site
Page 11, bottom: Courtesy of Hank Umemoto
Page 12: Courtesy of Shirley Nagatomi Okabe
Page 13, top: Photo by Charles E. Mace. Courtesy of The Bancroft Library, University of California, Berkeley.
Page 13, bottom: Photo by Marion Palfi. © 1998 Center for Creative Photography, Arizona Board of Regents. Marion Palfi, a Berlin-born social documentary photographer, took photos of Japanese American families at the Evergreen Hostel in 1946 as part of her Rosenwald Fellowship. Her emotional images are a striking contrast to the photos taken by the U.S. government of the resettlement of Japanese Americans. This print was donated to the County of Los Angeles Public Library by Jun Oyama, pictured on the far left.
Page 14: Photo by Charles E. Mace. Courtesy of The Bancroft Library, University of California, Berkeley.
Page 16: Courtesy of the Department of Special Collections/UCLA Charles E. Young Library/Daily News
Page 17: Toyo Miyatake Studio
Page 18: Courtesy of Sande Hashimoto and Little Tokyo Historical Society
Page 19: Toyo Miyatake Studio
Page 20: Photo by Dorothea Lange. Courtesy of The Bancroft Library, University of California, Berkeley.

Page 21, left: Japanese American National Museum (Gift of the Japanese American Medical Association, 2005.138)

Page 21, right: The Bancroft Library, University of California, Berkeley

Page 23, left and right: Photos by Dorothea Lange. Courtesy of The Bancroft Library, University of California, Berkeley.

Page 24: Courtesy of Janice D. Tanaka

Page 25: Courtesy of Janice D. Tanaka

Page 26, top: Photo by Charles E. Mace. Courtesy of The Bancroft Library, University of California, Berkeley.

Page 26, bottom: Courtesy of The Bancroft Library, University of California, Berkeley

Page 27: Photo from the family of Sue Kunitomi Embrey. Courtesy of Manzanar National Historic Site.

Page 29: Photo by Ansel Adams. Courtesy of the Library of Congress.

Page 31: Photo by Stone Ishimaru. Courtesy of The Bancroft Library, University of California, Berkeley. © Tec Com Productions.

Page 33: Courtesy of the family of Momo Nagano Kwong

Page 34: Collection of Heather C. Lindquist

Page 36, top: Courtesy of Irene Nagao Kaneshiki and Pauline Nagao Caulk

Page 36, bottom: Seabrook Educational and Cultural Center. Courtesy of Rutgers University Library.

Page 37: Seabrook Educational and Cultural Center

Page 39: Rose Hanawa Tanaka Collection, Manzanar National Historic Site

Page 41: Collection of Heather C. Lindquist

Page 42: Shades of LA Collection, Los Angeles Public Library. Permission granted by the family of Iku Kato Kiriyama.

Page 44, top: MOHAI, Seattle Post-Intelligencer Photograph Collection, P128050

Page 44, bottom right: Bainbridge Island Review Collection. Courtesy of Densho.

Page 44, bottom left: Hayashida Family Collection. Courtesy of Densho.

Page 45: Bainbridge Island Japanese American Community, the Kitamoto Family Collection. Courtesy of Densho.

Page 47: Photo by Tom Parker. Courtesy of The Bancroft Library, University of California, Berkeley. This image, part of the WRA's Photographic Section, was unusual because it included a note in Japanese, which began "Oh my! Three cute children." The source of this Japanese caption is unknown.

Page 51: Southern California Gardeners' Federation Collection. Courtesy of Naomi Hirahara.

Page 52: Japanese American National Museum (Photograph by Toyo Miyatake Studio, Gift of the Alan Miyatake Family, 96.267.204)

Chapter Two

Page 54: Toyo Miyatake Studio

Page 56: Photo by Archie Miyatake. Courtesy of Toyo Miyatake Studio.

Page 60: Japanese American National Museum (Photograph by Toyo Miyatake Studio, Gift of the Alan Miyatake Family, 96.267.318)

Page 61: Courtesy of Grace Fukumoto

Page 62: Los Angeles Examiner

Page 64: National Archives and Records Administration

Page 65: Courtesy of Grace Fukumoto

Page 66: Courtesy of ACLU San Diego

Page 67: Seabrook Farms Collection, RUcore (Rutgers University Community Repository), retrieved from https://doi.org/doi:10.7282/T3PV6MD1

Page 69: Seabrook Farms Collection, RUcore (Rutgers University Community Repository), retrieved from http://dx.doi.org/doi:10.7282/T39C6VWZ

Page 70: Paul T. Bannai

Page 72, top: Collection of Heather C. Lindquist

Page 72, bottom left: Courtesy of Cyndy Fujikawa

Page 72, bottom right: Courtesy of Jill Hatanaka

Page 73: Courtesy of Jill Hatanaka

Page 75: Photo by Dorothea Lange. Courtesy of The Bancroft Library, University of California, Berkeley.

Page 76: Photo from *The Red Angel: The Life and Times of Elaine Black Yoneda, 1906–1988,* by Vivian McGuckin Raineri (New York: International Publishers, 1991)

Page 81: Photo by Charles E. Mace. Courtesy of The Bancroft Library, University of California, Berkeley.

Page 83: General Motors

Page 84: "Wizard with Rocks" article and photographs © SEPS, licensed by Curtis Licensing, Indianapolis, IN. All rights reserved.

Page 86: Historic Images, https://www.historicimages.com

Page 88: Photo from the family of Sue Kunitomi Embrey. Courtesy of Manzanar National Historic Site.

Page 89: Photo from the family of Sue Kunitomi Embrey. Courtesy of Manzanar National Historic Site.

Page 92: "Torch 55" yearbook

Page 94: "Caerulea 5" yearbook

Chapter Three

Page 96: The Manzanar Committee

Page 99, left and right: Courtesy of Alan Nishio

Page 101: Gidra Collection. Courtesy of Densho.

Page 103, top and bottom: Evan Johnson Collection, Manzanar National Historic Site

Page 104: Gann Matsuda/The Manzanar Committee

Page 109: © Mary Uyematsu Kao, 2004

Page 111: Bob Fitch Photography Archive, Stanford University Libraries, photo item no. M1994

Page 114: Courtesy of John Tateishi

Page 116: Photo by Glen Kitayama. Courtesy of the NCRR.

Page 119: Courtesy of Aiko Herzig-Yoshinaga

Page 123: Photo by Susie Ling. Courtesy of Visual Communications.

Page 127: Photo by Kris Marubayashi. Courtesy of the Nikkei for Civil Rights and Redress Archives Collection.

Page 130: Photo by Crystal K. Huie. Courtesy of the Fred T. Korematsu Institute.

Page 131: Japanese American National Museum (Gift of Hannah Tomiko Holmes, 88.4.1B)

Page 132: Courtesy of the Nikkei for Civil Rights and Redress Archives Collection

Page 133: Courtesy of Yuriko Hohri

Chapter Four

Page 134: Photo by Matt Givot

Page 136: Armed Forces History Division, National Museum of American History, Smithsonian Institution

Page 139: Ron Izuno Collection, Manzanar National Historic Site

Page 140: Manzanar Committee Collection, Manzanar National Historic Site

Page 143: Photo by USMC Corporal Jason Ingersoll

Page 144: Photo by Lieutenant Colonel Randy Pullen. U.S. Department of Defense.

Page 146: Jason Millstein Photography

Page 147, left: Courtesy of Edgar Wakayama

Page 147, right: U.S. Department of Veterans Affairs, National Cemetery Administration

Page 148: Chloe Coleman/NPR

Page 150: Photo by Patrick T. Fallon

Page 154: Photo by Patrick T. Fallon

Epilogue

Page 156: Photo by Patrick T. Fallon

Page 158, top and bottom: Photos by Patrick T. Fallon

Page 159: Photo by Patrick T. Fallon

Page 160: Manzanar National Historic Site

Page 161: Photo by Matt Givot

Page 162: MARIO G. REYES/*Rafu Shimpo*

Page 163, right: Photo by Maria Kwong. Courtesy of the family of Momo Nagano Kwong.

Page 163, left: MARIO G. REYES/*Rafu Shimpo*

Page 165, top: The Bancroft Library, University of California, Berkeley

Page 165, middle: The Manzanar Project

Page 165, bottom: Courtesy of the Rolex Awards for Enterprise. Gordon Sato was selected as a Rolex Laureate in 2002.

Page 167: Sean Miura. The sign, created by Sean Miura and Tanzila Ahmed, is now part of the Smithsonian Museum of American History's collection.

Page 168, top and bottom: Photos by Patrick T. Fallon

Page 169: Daren Mooko

ABOUT THE AUTHORS

Naomi Hirahara is a writer of both nonfiction books and mysteries. With Geraldine Knatz, she cowrote *Terminal Island: The Lost Communities of Los Angeles Harbor*, which won a Bruckman Award for Excellence and an Award of Merit from the Conference of California Historical Societies. Her Edgar Award–winning *Mas Arai* mysteries have been published in France, Japan, and Korea. A former editor of the *Rafu Shimpo* newspaper, she also curates historical exhibitions and writes articles and short stories.

Heather C. Lindquist is the editor of *Children of Manzanar,* a co-publication by Heyday and Manzanar History Association, which received an award of excellence from the Association of Partners for Public Lands in 2013, and she was one of several contributing authors to *Freedom in My Heart: Voices from the United States National Slavery Museum,* published by *National Geographic* in 2007. She has also written numerous exhibit scripts for museums, visitor centers, and national parks across the country, including Manzanar National Historic Site; the National Prisoner of War Museum at Andersonville, Georgia; the Natural History Museum of Los Angeles County; and the Museum of Science and Industry in Chicago.

HEYDAY
into California

About Heyday

Heyday is an independent, nonprofit publisher and unique cultural institution. We promote widespread awareness and celebration of California's many cultures, landscapes, and boundary-breaking ideas. Through our well-crafted books, public events, and innovative outreach programs we are building a vibrant community of readers, writers, and thinkers.

Thank You

It takes the collective effort of many to create a thriving literary culture. We are thankful to all the thoughtful people we have the privilege to engage with. Cheers to our writers, artists, editors, storytellers, designers, printers, bookstores, critics, cultural organizations, readers, and book lovers everywhere!

We are especially grateful for the generous funding we've received for our publications and programs during the past year from foundations and hundreds of individual donors. Major supporters include:

Anonymous (5); John Atwood, in memory of Jeanne Carevic; Judith and Phillip Auth; Judy Avery; Carroll Ballard and Christina Lüscher-Ballard; Richard and Rickie Ann Baum; BayTree Fund; Robert Joseph Bell and Gwendolyn Wynne; Jean and Fred Berensmeier; Joan Berman; Nancy Bertelsen; Joan Bingham; Edwin Blue; Teresa Book and Steve Wax, in memory of Saul Alinsky; Beatrice Bowles; Philip and Jamie Bowles, in memory of Mike McCone; Peter Boyer and Terry Gamble Boyer; John Briscoe; California State Library; The Campbell Foundation; The Christensen Fund; The City of Berkeley; Lawrence Crooks; H. Dwight Damon, in memory of Jim Houston; Bruce De Benedictis and Caroline Kim; Meera Desai; Chris Desser and Kirk Marckwald; Frances Dinkelspiel and Gary Wayne; Steven Dinkelspiel; Tim Disney; Patricia

Board of Directors

Getting Involved

To learn more about our publications, events, and other ways you can participate, please visit www.heydaybooks.com.

This material received Federal financial assistance for the preservation and interpretation of U.S. confinement sites where Japanese Americans were detained during World War II. Under Title VI of the Civil Rights Act of 1964, Section 504 of the Rehabilitation Act of 1973, and the Age Discrimination Act of 1975, as amended, the U.S. Department of the Interior prohibits discrimination on the basis of race, color, national origin, disability or age in its federally funded assisted projects. If you believe you have been discriminated against in any program, activity, or facility as described above, or if you desire further information, please write to: Office of Equal Opportunity, National Park Service, 1849 C Street, NW, Washington, DC 20240.